D1187757

PAUL SCOTT: IMAGES OF INDIA

Paul Scott, Images of India

Patrick Swinden

It was a survival of exiles. Their enemy was light, not dark, the light of their own kind, of their own people at home from whom they had been too long cut off so that, returning there briefly, a deep and holy silence wrapped them and caused them to observe what was real as miniature. In India they had been betrayed by an illusion of topographical vastness into sins of pride that were foreign to their insular, pygmy natures.

The Day of the Scorpion, II, ii, 4

First published 1980 by
THE MACMILLAN PRESS LTD
London and Basingstoke
Companies and representatives
throughout the world

Printed in Hong Kong

British Library Cataloguing in Publication Data

Swinden, Patrick
   Paul Scott, images of India
   1. Scott, Paul – Criticism and interpretation
   I. Title
   823'.9'14   PR6069.C596Z/

   ISBN 0-333-27740-6

For Serena

Contents

Preface

Three years ago I had never heard of Paul Scott. Then, in November 1977, he won the Booker prize for fiction; and a few words about him and his novel *Staying On* appeared in the newspapers. These included a brief comment, sympathetic and admiring, by Philip Larkin, who was one of the judges. Less than six months later he was dead.

Puzzled by the Booker award and saddened by news of Scott's death so soon afterwards, I decided I should have a look at one of his books. I had been given to understand that his largest achievement was a tetralogy about the last days of the Raj in India, so I started on a reading of the first novel in the series, *The Jewel in the Crown*. On finishing the first Part of this long book, 'Miss Crane', I was convinced that I had encountered a novelist of major stature. Nothing I have read of his since has made me change my mind. Rather I was shocked that it had taken the death of an author fifty-seven years old, with thirteen published novels to his credit, to make me recognise his existence.

There is a moral in this. When I looked for Paul Scott's books in public libraries, I discovered that most of them were on the borrowed list. When I went into the bookshops, I found that almost all the paperback volumes of the *Raj Quartet* had been sold, and replacements were on order. When I went into the university library to check the stocks, I saw not a single novel by Paul Scott in the shelves or the catalogues. In other words I was not alone in my ignorance. But it was an ignorance shared mainly by academics, not ordinary members of the general reading public. Yet Scott's novels had been, for some time, well received by reviewers – though the only extensive commentary on his work that I could find in a public journal was Max Beloff's long review of the *Raj Quartet* in *Encounter* (to which I refer at the opening of my chapter on the *Quartet*).

I have written this book for three reasons: to alleviate my sense of guilt at failing to notice the work of a fine writer before he died; to draw the attention of other people professionally concerned with literature to the great merit of Paul Scott's fiction; and to try to encourage a wider public to read (and it seems it will often be the case reread) some of these splendid novels.

There is so much to admire in Paul Scott's work that one is aware that many gaps will be revealed in one's appreciation of it, especially in a short book like this. But now is not the time for long, painstaking analyses of the novels. What is required is a brief but, I hope, thoughtful and enthusiastic treatment of them. Most of the general reasons for my admiration will appear in the introduction to this book, and in the chapters that follow on the individual novels. As a word of encouragement to the wary reader, however, I should like to take this opportunity to suggest two of those reasons in bold outline.

First, there is the consistency of Scott's achievement. With the possible exception of *The Bender*, he has not written a single novel which is not a fully serious and accomplished work of fiction. As he gets into his stride the scope of his interest widens, the depth of his understanding of human nature becomes more profound, and his technical resources grow more sophisticated as the subjects on which they are brought to bear grow more complex. But his first published novel, *Johnnie Sahib*, is, within its own terms of reference (which are less narrow than its subject might lead one to suppose), highly accomplished and well written throughout.

Second, there is the completeness of his achievement. On receiving the Booker prize Scott said: 'I have finished with India for ever. It just needed some little valedictory thing' (i.e. *Staying On*). No one can say what fresh subject would have claimed his attention had he survived his fifty-eighth year. But that confession does indicate something that must surely be felt by the author and his readers alike: that *Staying On* represents the end of a long and important phase in Scott's career as a writer. In my view, the thirteen novels as a whole add up to a finished achievement, with everything said that needed to be said about the interesting and varied subjects Scott had chosen to write about so far. The *Quartet*, especially, demonstrates that he had acquired as complete a mastery as one could legitimately expect of an approach to the writing of fiction he had been developing over the previous twenty-five years.

I should like to thank friends and relatives with whom I have discussed Paul Scott's work. Special thanks are owed to Judith Brown, whose intimate and extensive knowledge of Indian politics during the Independence period has prevented me from making several errors of fact. Also to M. R. Elliott-Bateman, for information he provided about the military aspect of the Anglo-Indian situation in Burma and Malaya during and immediately after the Second World War. Any mistakes that remain are my own responsibility. Penny Evans went to great trouble preparing the typescript. My wife, Serena, whose interest in the novels began at the same time as my own, has been a mine of information and ideas; and deserves at least half the credit for whatever is satisfactory in this book.

The author and publishers wish to thank the following who have kindly given permission for the use of copyright material: David Higham Associates Ltd on behalf of the Estate of Paul Scott for extracts from *The Birds of Paradise*, *Staying On*, *The Alien Sky*, *A Division of the Spoils*, *Johnnie Sahib*, *The Chinese Love Pavilion*, *The Mark of the Warrior*, *The Jewel in the Crown*, *A Male Child*, *The Day of the Scorpion*, and *The Corrida at San Felíu*; and the Trustees of the Joseph Conrad Estate for an extract from *Lord Jim*.

NOTE: In his Indian novels, Scott uses the term 'Eurasian' to describe a person who is the offspring of a mixed marriage between European and Asian parents. He uses the word 'Anglo-Indian' to describe the offspring of a mixed marriage between English and Indian parents. And he has a number of ways of referring to the British in India, 'British-Indian' being the most frequently used. I have tried to simplify things by using the word 'Eurasian' to denote any person who is the offspring of a mixed marriage in Malaya, Burma, or India; reserving the word 'Anglo-Indian' for the English (and other British residents) in India, in the sense in which it is commonly used – e.g. by George Orwell in his essay on Kipling. I think the advantages outweigh the disadvantages, especially the awkward substitution of 'British-Indian' for the less precise but more familiar 'Anglo-Indian' in the context of British rule in India.

Scott's novels can be read either in hardcover (Heinemann) or in paperback (Panther) editions. These have different page references and so when I quote from the text I provide references

I Paradise Lost: an Introduction

[The birds of Paradise] were brought to me the same day they were caught and I had an opportunity of examining them in all their beauty and vivacity. As soon as I found they were generally brought alive, I set one of my men to make a large bamboo cage with troughs of food and water, hoping to be able to keep some of them . . . They drank plenty of water and were in constant motion, jumping about the cage from perch to perch, clinging to the top and the sides, and rarely resting a moment . . . The second day they were always less active . . . and on the morning of the third day they were almost always found dead at the bottom of the cage, without apparent cause.

Alfred Russel Wallace, *The Malay Archipelago* (quoted in Book III
of *The Birds of Paradise*)

Both all things vain, and all who in vain things
Built thir fond hopes of Glorie or lasting fame,
Or happiness in this or th'other life;
All who have thir reward on Earth, the fruits
Of painful Superstition and blind Zeal,
Nought seeking but the praise of men, here find
Fit retribution, emptie as thir deeds; . . .

Milton, *Paradise Lost*, III, ll, 448–54

To claim that Paul Scott's novels are about the loss of Paradise is to suggest an unusually high ambition and, perhaps, a correspondingly dangerous naivety. But it is not unusual for writers

to embark on a quest for Paradise and to see it fall further below
the horizon the nearer to the horizon they sail. It is not unusual
for them to watch Paradise subtly transform itself into a more
questionable shape the nearer it is approached, the more closely
it is investigated; to witness a glorious illusion fading into a reality
more impeachable, less exalting to the spirit, sometimes profoundly destructive of the aspiration, even the very character, of
the man who sought to enter it.

Paul Scott's Paradise has never been other than illusory. From
the beginning of his career as a novelist he has been preoccupied
with Paradises that are already lost, and he has sought to bring
his characters to terms with that loss. He has tried to make them
recognise the illusory nature of the ambitions that drive them and
the desires that perplex them. This preoccupation with what men
most want for themselves, what they want to believe in, or, more
subtly what they want to suppose they *have* believed in, makes
Scott a difficult writer. Difficult because of the often complex
states of mind many of his characters possess, and difficult
because of the way those states of mind shift and change under
the pressure of what are often extraordinary experiences. In the
novels we discover people engaged in a struggle with circumstances they will usually fail to understand, and instead reconstruct
in the image of their own ambitions and desires. That is why the
stage of his fiction is so often populated by the obsessed, the
deranged, the hypocritical, and the intensely self-deceived.

The illusory world so many of Scott's characters inhabit is the
consequence, in a way not easy to define, of their author's
fascination with India. His fiction needs to be sustained by events
in the Indian sub-continent between 1942 and 1947. This is the
span of time that is traversed gradually, shiftingly, with many
halts and retrospects, in the *Raj Quartet*. It is also the place and the
period in which the events of all Scott's other successful novels
take place. Even when the setting is a tiny island in the East
Indies and the time long after the ending of the war in the East (in
The Birds of Paradise) the real impetus of the novel springs from
the India between the wars and its transformation into a post-
war independent state. The fighting in Malaya that provides the
background of *The Chinese Love Pavilion* is a consequence of the
defence of India from Japanese invasion. Even in Scott's one
successful and important novel which deals with events outside

India and the war altogether (*The Corrida at San Felíu*), events in India, at Mahwar and Darshansingh, play a significant part in the construction of the plot.

Yet Paul Scott had not been abroad, let alone to India, until he was over twenty years old. Although his novels leave us with the impression of a man thoroughly at home with his Indian subject (and no less at home with it for being critical of his countrymen's attitudes towards it) he knew nothing of India beyond what a few books had told him before he volunteered for service in the Indian Army. Then he was commissioned in India, and was posted to an air supply unit which took him to Burma and Malaya. (One wonders about his relation to Scottie, in *Johnnie Sahib*, who is a Captain in just such a unit operating in Burma in 1944.) He remained in India only until 1946, when he returned to England. For the most part he lived in England ever since, with occasional visits to India mainly for the purpose of collecting or checking material in the novels.

Paul Scott was born in 1920 in Palmers Green, North London, the second son of a family of commercial artists. His father appears to have been only moderately successful. Scott's origins were therefore humbly professional middle class. He was educated at Winchmore Hill Collegiate and later, at his father's insistence, he began training as an accountant, until he was called up in 1940. He began his national service as a non-commissioned officer in Intelligence and remained there, in the UK, for three years. His commission in the Indian Army came with his arrival in India in 1943. But a year after his war service was completed, in 1946, he was demobilised and returned to England. There he was appointed secretary to the Falcon and Grey Walls Press, a publishing company run by the Labour MP Peter Baker. He left Baker's company in 1950 to become a literary agent with David Higham Associates Limited. For ten years he was a director of the company, and produced four novels, from *Johnnie Sahib* to *The Mark of the Warrior* (1958). Then he resigned his position (in 1960) to become a freelance writer. He did not acquire a large following as a novelist until the *Raj Quartet* was well under way, in the early 1970s; and real popularity only came with the publication of *Staying On*, which won the Booker Prize in 1977. He died on 1 March 1978.

Scott appears to have been a very private man. There are no

tantalising snippets of information about him in the literary magazines. Indeed there is little about his books either – in spite of the wide readership they are attracting now. He apparently loved music and the cinema as much as he loved literature. He married, in 1941, Nancy Edith Avery, by whom he had two daughters. These are mere fragments of information, and he would be a foolish man who in present circumstances sought to make available the details of Scott's life, in a biographical study. My own purpose is quite different. It is to inquire about the position of India as a country and an idea in the mind of a man who, on the surface, had so little to do with it. What it meant to him we can surmise from the way he wrote about it. What it means to his characters is, I think, an altogether different thing.

In Scott's novels India is the supreme illusion. Here, for many of his characters, is Paradise. Or, if not Paradise, a setting for their lives which they feel can be replaced by nothing else. They have defined themselves, their duties, their professions, their moral values, their habits of social behaviour and personal assessment, in relation to India. Scott shows that for the British who lived there India was an all-embracing experience. Their minds admitted only dim recollections of 'home' in England. The houses and gardens of the Home Counties to which they were sent away to be educated, and from which they returned to take up positions as soldiers and administrators, had to be transplanted in a different climate and a more spacious geography.

The Anglo-Indian response to England is nowhere better explained in Scott's work than by Sarah Layton in the second volume of the *Quartet*. Sarah looks at England through the perspective of her Indian childhood, though in the passage that follows she is walking through an English meadow, in the direction of a brook – which reminds her of another brook back in India near her father's military cantonment:

The brook babbling over the stones reminded her of Pankot in miniature. But then everything in England was on a miniature scale. She thought this had an effect on the people who lived there always. In comparison with her mother . . . Aunt Lydia [who returned to England permanently, unlike her sisters Fenny and Mildred] seemed to Sarah to lack a dimension the

others didn't lack. Lacking this dimension was what Sarah
supposed came of living on a tiny island.

The Day of the Scorpion, i, ii, 3

People like Sarah Layton and her family have no option but to
allow their vision and expectations to develop within the Indian
dimension, to adjust themselves to a scale against which the
landscapes of England appear as miniatures. Living in England
will be as unnatural to Sarah as she is later to suppose living in
India, that is to say living in the new Independent India, would
be. In some ways more so, since the sense of physical scale and
proportion has a great deal to do with belonging, a great deal to
do with the cultivation and assertion of a personal identity.

It is the triumph of the *Quartet* as a whole, and it is the triumph
to a lesser extent of many of Scott's other novels, that he has fully
understood, almost one might say shared, the illusion of India,
the Englishman's India. He has given it a density, an animation,
a capacity for movement and alteration, an ability to be looked at
from many sides, experienced through a variety of points of view,
which can be true only of something that possesses a certain
reality. Indeed, reality of a kind must come into being when a
landscape and a people are subjected to the creative pressure of so
many minds, differing in any number of important ways, but
ultimately controlled by an intangible idea of the rightness of
their presence – more than that, their *superior* presence – in the
place they now call home. But Scott has also understood the
impermanence of this reality. He has understood that when this
impermanence is not recognised by those whose reality it is felt to
be then the reality, however substantial or laden with the histories
and emblems of those who have lived it, itself becomes an illusion.

The men and women Scott is interested in are of two opposite
kinds: those who foster the illusion of permanence most strenu-
ously; and those who are beginning to recognise the illusion
for what it really is. He is most interested in the second kind,
because to feel as they do is to lose a part, perhaps a very large
part, of their own reality – which has been over so many years
dependent upon their connection with India. How is a man to
hold on to a sense of personal reality when he can feel the external
props which have sustained it for so long, at first gently, and then
violently, being pulled away? This is the dominant theme of

Scott's fiction. A sense of personal integration and belonging is a sort of Paradise. To feel it falling apart, under the combined pressure of an external threat and a private capitulation to what the threat has exposed in the self that is threatened, is of necessity to experience a loss of Paradise.

The *Raj Quartet* is Scott's most complete history of this process. Here, the demise of British India is traced through the fortunes of an enormous cast of characters who respond to these problems of personal identity in a variety of ways. But from his earliest work, Scott has sought to expose the characters in his fiction to the collapse of their illusions and the consequent threat administered to their sense of personal identity.

For this reason, and because he has absorbed himself so completely in the fortunes of his characters, we cannot count Scott among the merely documentary novelists of the end of the Empire. To document the stages of the British withdrawal from India would alone have been an enormous task for a novelist to perform. But Scott has done much more than that. He has produced a picture of human activity which is only very slightly dependent on the reader's pre-existent interest in Anglo-Indian politics and society during the 1940s. In other words the *variety* of his work, let alone its searching commitment to the human struggle, is remarkable. I should like to enumerate, briefly, some of the facts about it which lead me to use that word.

In so far as the characters are concerned, Scott's early novels are remarkable for the insight they show into male psychology. He has in common with Conrad and Kipling an ability to create convincing pictures of men at work, subject to the strain of conflicting responsibilities but also involved in the practical business of getting on with a job – whether that involves loading aircraft with supplies of ammunition, or running a model farm, or governing a province. Scott never underestimates the importance of work as a context within which the men in his novels enter into their emotional involvements, and this work is usually work in the sense that is commonly understood by the word, i.e. not some kind of artistic or literary profession. However, when he does place a writer at the centre of a novel – in the *Corrida at San Feliu* – he produces a very plausible account of problems that arise from the business of being a novelist. Also, in his handling of conversation between men Scott usually manages to avoid both of the traps many of his contemporaries fall into: a disembodied, neutered exchange of judgements and opinions; or an aggressive verbal onslaught liberally interlaced with four-letter words and other disparaging sexual references. (Compare the recently much-admired *Middle Parts of Fortune* by Frederic Manning with *Johnnie Sahib* – both about soldiers in a virtually all-male environment – in this respect.)

The male ambiance of much of Scott's early work is immediately recognisable and unusually convincing during a period of literary history in which one or other of the less desirable alternatives has transformed too many male characters into squeamish nonentities or sex-crazed boors. On the other hand only the least satisfactory of these novels contain female characters drawn in depth. One of these, *A Male Child*, is in any case mainly preoccupied with a male sibling relationship. The other, *The Alien Sky*, gives a much more prominent position to a woman. Dorothy Gower is the only female character in the pre-*Quartet* novels to be given as important a role to play as any of the men. Her situation is an interesting one, and her character is explored with some subtlety – as I shall try to show – but in the end Scott doesn't manage to give as clear a picture of her as he does, say, of Johnnie Brown or Ian Canning, or even Major Craig in *The Mark of the Warrior*. Women in the later novels (before the *Quartet*) tend to be mysterious (Teena Chang in *The Chinese Love Pavilion*), idealised figures from the past (Dora in *The Birds of Paradise*) or not altogether convincingly eccentric (Anina in *The Bender*). Anne, William Conway's wife in *The Birds of Paradise*, is a sign of better things to come, but she is given very little space to develop during the flashbacks that describe the breakdown of Conway's marriage with her in that novel. Also Myra Thornhill, in *The Corrida*, is a plausible character, though the concentration on her husband's work and fortunes restricts the scope of our interest in her too.

Certainly there is little in the earlier novels to prepare us for the startlingly penetrating and varied presentation of the female characters in the *Quartet*. There, the Layton family alone supplies us with several fully developed portraits of women: Susan and Sarah, their mother Mildred, and the two aunts, Lydia and Fenny. Daphne Manners plays a central role in the first book, and Barbie Batchelor does the same in the third. Also in the third book, there is the picture of the memsahibs of Pankot, each of them subtly different from the others and adopting slightly different attitudes to the raj ideal upheld at the administrative and governmental levels by their menfolk. That is to say nothing of other female characters who play important parts during certain phases of the action: Lady Manners, Lili Chatterjee, Edwina Crane, and Sister Ludmila. The cast is extraordinarily varied: old, young and middle-aged; happily and unhappily married; attached and unattached; in their public and private circumstances. It is not surprising that, coming to the last novel from the completed *Quartet*, we should find there an equal distribution of emphasis on the male and female sides of a single marriage. Lucy Smalley is one of the most lively characters in the whole of contemporary English fiction.

The best novels do not succeed through character alone – important, even pre-eminent, though the presentation of character must be. People live in places, which exist in their own right with distinctive textures, colours, salients and declivities, weathers and physical contours. Scott is alert to all these aspects of landscape – and city-scape too. He is sensitive to their physical features. Sensitive also to the way they change in different atmospheric conditions, and when people travel across them from different directions, with different purposes and expectations about what they will find and in what circumstances they will find it. He is aware of the habit landscapes have of gathering into themselves the feelings of people who are aware of them, who notice them. And so he registers very accurately the inter-penetration of human activity and the surfaces upon which that activity takes place, the topographical backdrop (which therefore becomes more than a backdrop) against which it proceeds.

One reason for this is the remarkable way in which Scott varies his point of view so that we experience an event from within a community which is affected by it; and then at other times we view the same event or a related event more impartially – through the eyes of someone not directly concerned with it, possibly hostile or at least indifferent to the community of which we once felt ourselves to be a part. This is a conspicuous feature of the *Quartet*. There, our involvement in an event described in any one long section of narrative seems to exclude for the time being our interest in anything that might appear or have appeared in any other. The description of Edwina Crane's experiences during the disturbances of August 1942, in the first Part of *The Jewel in the Crown*, is so absorbing, so completely demanding of our attention, that the move to the MacGregor House in Part Two is a considerable wrench. Only gradually are the links forged in our minds that bind the events that happen there to the very different events that have preceded them, and that help to explain them.

There are many other devices which roughen the texture of the narrative and give it the variety and density which Scott became more and more adept at creating the closer he came to the *Quartet*. One other of them which I think should be mentioned at this stage, because Scott's manipulation of it is so deftly original, is the attention he pays to objects–articles of clothing, tools, keepsakes, weapons, anything that can be held in the hand or worn over a part of the body. Of course all successful novelists are attentive to the possessions as well as the dispositions of their characters, some going so far as to conspire with their characters to hoard and tabulate whatever they own or covet or acquire. Scott's handling of objects as contributions to the narrative is rather different from this, though. He has an intuitive gift for noticing how, through use or transaction, loss or discovery, these objects are felt to carry a significance much in excess of their obvious value or utility. The relationship between people and objects can be mysteriously symbiotic. Something about the object influences the behaviour of a character or affects the way we, as readers, feel about him. Such an object is felt to carry a significance which will vary in its relation to one character or another, a significance which will be enlarged or diminished in the light of its history, its circulation among the *dramatis personae*. Certainly this interest in the 'psychological' value of objects increases markedly after the first four novels, and becomes a distinctive feature of the *Quartet*. In my chapters on the later novels I shall emphasise the way Scott uses objects to bring together in the reader's mind characters who are far apart, indeed who may never come into contact with one another, except by proxy: through the transference from the one to the other, by often devious and untraceable pathways, of such objects as a Malayan dagger, a caged bird, a lace christening shawl, or a book of Urdu poems.

2 The Early Novels

Why had he sat thus? Because he was afraid? What had been
his fear? Fear of being watched? Fear of what lay in the air,
invisibly ready to spring? Yes – this; and something else. There
had been still was – he felt fingers of it tugging inside him now –
a formlessness, an almost negative despair which was at once
part of him and outside him, suspending and sustaining him
between two worlds as it were. Only there were never two
worlds. There was one world and one world only. And in it one
had one's place or had no place.

The Alien Sky, II, 3

JOHNNIE SAHIB (1952)

The first of Scott's thirteen novels, *Johnnie Sahib*, was sent to
seventeen publishers before it was accepted by Eyre &
Spottiswoode and published in 1952. This is surprising. *Johnnie*
was a war novel written at a time when war novels were very
much in vogue both in Britain and America. Also the background of the story in Wingate's operations in Burma in 1943–44
was one of the few episodes of the British contribution to the war
in the Far East in which an English reader might be expected to
take a patriotic interest. The narrative is straightforward and
uncomplicated by reminiscence or any other form of temporal
displacement. On the other hand the lack of romantic interest,
and the fact that we never get near the front-line fighting (no shot
being fired by accident, let alone in anger) might have something
to do with publishing houses' reluctance to handle the book.
Nevertheless, in spite of a certain thinness compared with much
of Scott's later fiction, *Johnnie Sahib* has much to recommend it.
Several of the themes of his work have already emerged with
some force and clarity.

The story of Johnnie Brown is a part of the story of how the British and American troops swept through Burma from Comitarla, Prulli, Tamel and Pyongui. The stages of the advance south are represented by the five 'Parts' into which the novel is divided. In Comitarla an air supply outfit is being run very professionally, but on a small scale, by a major (whose surname we are never given). He is responsible for three company sections, one of which is headed by Johnnie Brown, the charismatic but potentially irresponsible Sahib of the title.

The novel opens with two visitors to Comitarla who are to affect profoundly the fortunes of the Major's company in general and Johnnie and his section in particular. The first is Lieutenant-Colonel Baxter from Calcutta, who is on a mission of inspection prior to setting the whole air-to-ground operation on a wider, less casual and personal basis. The second is Lieutenant Jim Taylor, a replacement for Johnnie's ex-second-in-command. When Johnnie goes on leave and the company sets off for Prulli, Taylor finds his command of Section 3 compromised by the mystique of their absent leader and the Major's clumsy method of helping him to dispel it. In the meantime the Major is trying to reconcile himself to the new dispositions coming through from Baxter. He is also trying to get the men to adapt to the different kind of company relationship which he feels has to follow from the enlargement of the military operation. The strain of this responsibility has a damaging effect on his dealings with Johnnie when he returns. It drives a wedge of suspicion not merely between himself and Johnnie, but also between Johnnie and Jim Taylor. This feeds the men's disaffection, in the enlarged and reorganised supply operation Baxter has created (an operation that is now called RAMO – Rear Airfield Maintenance Organisation). Eventually Johnnie's impatience with the impersonal scale of operations, and his carelessness over paperwork, force the Major to take his section away from him and send him back to base at Marapore. The effect of this on the men under him, and on Taylor and the Major, constitute the main substance of the last two Parts of the book.

The novel, then, is less about the actual fighting in Burma (there isn't a single Japanese character in it) than about the often humdrum operations necessary to the fighting that is going on elsewhere. Most of the work consists of transferring ammunition

from the dump at Prulli or Tamel to the British and American
planes that have landed in jungle air-strips behind the front line.
The main issues have to do with men at work. As Scott has said of
this novel: 'These men are running a business. True, the dividend
for the shareholders is survival, but as in any other business that
was ever run that consideration is not necessarily the one in the
minds of the management. Other things seem just as serious at the
time.'

In this novel what seem serious at the time are the tempera-
mental differences between the men; differences that spring from
the day-to-day business of running the airfields, and later from
the absorption of the sections into the company and the company
into the overall pattern of Baxter's mechanisation of the supply
operations. All the men are caught in a conflict of interests in
which their pride in their own methods runs up against the need
for a more conventional strategy to achieve total defeat of the
Japanese. The Major recognises the inevitability of Baxter and
RAMO at the same time as he regrets the disintegration of his
company which it must involve. Johnnie, on the other hand, with
his more short-sighted view of the war, and almost mystical belief
in his section, fails to recognise what should be the limits of his
hitherto highly effective egotism. When Taylor takes over
command of his section he cannot reproduce the close bond of
fellowship Johnnie has forged with the men, men whom Johnnie
had chosen personally back in India years before:

> He [Johnnie] remembered . . . the electric shock of recog-
> nition that passed through his own body as his hand clapped a
> shoulder so that it seemed that another reached and touched
> his own. On that hot, parched afternoon there had been no
> uncertainty, no heartfelt fear for the future or regret for the
> past, only the direct communication between himself and the
> men he picked. Wherever he was with them, even now, the
> communication remained. It was always there, solid and
> dependable; there for the asking; there, comforting in the
> background, even without the asking.   *J.S.*, 1, 2

Scottie, the head of Section 2, doesn't try to emulate Johnnie's
success. He substitutes a gift of statistical calculation for Johnnie's
close communion with the men under his leadership. In the end it

is not surprising that it is Taylor and Scottie who are marked up
for promotion, and Johnnie who is deprived of his section, of the
men on whom he had seemed to depend for his outward charisma
and inward sense of male self-satisfaction. As the military
machine is gradually assembled for the final advance, there is no
room for the man who cannot separate his personality from his
job. As the Major says to him:

> You've been a binder. You haven't fitted in. But you've done
> your job, in your way. I don't mind a man not fitting in but his
> job's got to fit in, and your's doesn't any more. *J.S.*, III, 12

On this note Johnnie disappears from the book, about two-thirds
of the way through it. His only later appearance is made
indirectly in a brief letter to Jan Mohammed, one of his Indian
subordinates. Of course the influence of Johnnie persists long
after his actual disappearance. Nevertheless one is inclined to
wonder whether Scott has not risked too much by excluding him
from almost half of the novel. (He is on French leave at the
opening, when Baxter arrives for the first time, and he spends
most of Part II on leave whilst the arguments between Taylor
and the men and Taylor and the Major, occupy the foreground.)
On the other hand, the magnetism of Johnnie's personality when
he is present is very powerful. This is shown vividly in the scene in
which one of his Indian officers, Dass, comes to Johnnie to make a
complaint and finds himself in the presence of Taylor, the very
man he had intended to complain about. The way Johnnie offers
him an alternative reason for making this appointment (his
daughter is ill) shows considerable tact, an intimate knowledge of
the psychology of his men. It has the effect of satisfying honour on
all sides. There are other incidents which convince us about
Johnnie's air of authority, his legitimate expectation of respect;
also about his naivety, a certain immaturity on which his close,
often physical relation with the men is based.

With Johnnie absent for so much of the time, and Taylor's
difficulties with the men filling so much of the narrative, it is
natural that the character of the Major should absorb a great
deal of our attention. It could be argued that his is the most
interesting moral predicament in the novel, because he is more
deeply conscious of the terms of the struggle in which he is

engaged than any of the other characters are. Not only does he understand the logistics of the situation that Baxter has brought into being. He also understands what the consequences of the situation that has arisen are likely to be, for himself *and* for his company. Long before Baxter introduced the new dispensation, the Major had understood the very different effect his relationship with his company must have on himself from the one Johnnie Brown enjoys so unthinkingly with his men. For the Major:

> His individuality had gone; he was but a reflection of six other men; and a reflection of himself. His every action was dictated by majority will . . . And he was suddenly afraid because he felt there was no loneliness equal to that which comes when a man realises he no longer exists separately as a man; that to rule demands sacrifices, the greatest of all sacrifices; that he has ruled; that he has sacrificed; and is now nothing.   *J.S.*, ii, 5

This is an attitude to military responsibility displayed by several of Scott's characters elsewhere, notably Major Reid in *The Chinese Love Pavilion*. It tends particularly to be a cast of mind entered into by men of relatively humble origins who have risen to the middle ranks (in both of these cases the man is an army major). What follows from the Major's sense of anonymity, his lack of personal identity, is an intense feeling of duty to the men, a need to make it possible for them to avoid the sense of impersonality and isolation that his responsibility for them has nurtured in himself. He supposes that:

> Men were not connected. There was no communication between them. Sometimes a duplication of action or desire would make it seem as if it existed. But it was only there superficially, emotionally. It didn't go deeply to connect up the separate cores of their isolation.   *J.S.*, iii, 12

This runs counter to everything Johnnie's relationship with his men has encouraged him to believe in. What happens after he has been sent back to Marapore (as well as the way Taylor was treated by the men while Johnnie was on leave) renders Scott's final judgement uncertain. But there is a strong sense that the

Major is enunciating the more mature point of view, and that
Johnnie's charismatic effect on the men springs from a mutual
need that can be satisfied only in certain conditions – which are
impermanent and which will need to be transformed to meet new
challenges, changed situations. The core of isolation seems to lie
deeper than the sense of connection. This may have been more
than 'a duplication of action and desire', but it was almost
certainly less than the permanent condition of reciprocal respect
Johnnie had expected to last for ever.

Baxter's reconstruction of the air-supply organisation has
removed the conditions in which Johnnie's values can continue
to be of use. The reality of Comitarla has become the illusion of
Mandalay. It remains a vivid presence in the minds of some of the
soldiers, but the time and the place for its realisation in action
have passed. It has become a manifestation of the lost Paradise,
sealed off, in this novel, from the larger loss that the operation of
which it was a part was seeking to avert.

From the beginning, in a novel which has more the air of a
documentary about it than any of his other books, Scott has
emphasised many of the themes that are to preoccupy him in the
later fiction. No other of his books will be so unremittingly
concerned with men at work, but the work that men do will
usually figure importantly in whatever description of their
destinies and their inner lives constitutes the subject. This is one
of many respects in which Scott's representation of the British in
India differs from that of E. M. Forster. Forster's administrators
are scarcely ever seen doing anything essentially concerned with
administration. They organise a bridge party and subsequently
find that the plot demands that they conduct a trial. Ronnie
Heaslop says a few words about his civil responsibilities. But no
one would get the impression from a reading of *A Passage to India*
that the English ever really exerted themselves to rule India.
Even Fielding, who is not involved in the untouchable business of
administration, is never allowed to be seen teaching anybody in
his college. The place is simply a building for Mrs Moore and
Adela Quested to look around and pass comments upon.

Scott almost invariably enters the lives of his characters from
the opposite end of the work–leisure spectrum. First and foremost
his characters have to earn a living. In the process of earning a
living they create for themselves needs and ambitions out of

which the plots of their novels will grow. The *Raj Quartet* opens with the history of Edwina Crane and traces her career in the Mission schools to the stage at which she becomes Superintendent of the schools at Ranpur. We see her teaching the children in the classroom and organising the schools' programmes at the institutions of the teachers under her authority. Her character is formed very largely out of the problems she has to deal with in her profession. By contrast George Spruce (in *The Bender*) is an anomaly in Scott's fiction because a small annuity from a distant relative has allowed him to rub along without having to work at all. This is a situation which wrecks George's chances of leading a life in which he can take much satisfaction. It commits him to the role of comic picaresque hero, which, as countless novels of the 1950s might have warned, removes from him any significant trace of moral seriousness and psychological density.

Work, then, in Scott's fiction, is a very important context for characters to exist in; and the novelist who comes closest to Scott in this, as in several other respects, is not Forster but Conrad. In both novelists men find themselves in their work. The exigencies of their work often have much to do with the formation of their moral characters and with bringing out the peculiar qualities of their psychological strengths or weaknesses.

This is what is shown in the portrayal of Johnnie and the Major in *Johnnie Sahib*. It is the work on the airfield that provides Johnnie and Jim Taylor with their opportunities for success or failure with the men under their command. It is their attitude towards what they judge to be their success or failure at work which allows relationships to develop that provide the narrative with a plot. Similarly the Major's responsibility for his company, bringing him into conflict with Johnnie not over abstract principles, but over the actual details of the 'turn around' and the deployment of the men on the airstrips, is a function of his working life. It affects the direction of the narrative by virtue of that fact.

Important aspects of the characters of the two men, as they are tested in the work they perform and the way they exercise their responsibility, reappear and are explored more thoroughly and more subtly in the later novels. Johnnie's assumption that there is an intrinsic meaning and value in his relationship with the men contrasts with the Major's withdrawal from personal satisfaction, even from a sense of stable personal identity, in the interests of the larger context of the operation for which he is responsible. In the suspension of judgement over the attitudes of the two men it is possible to sense Scott's passionate concern with how lives are given meaning and how absolute the meanings given can ever be.

The Major's pessimistic view seems to have been shared by an otherwise quite dissimilar character, in *The Birds of Paradise*. There, William Conway imagines that his father prevented him from making a career in India not merely because he had anticipated the consequences of Independence (particularly on the Princely States in which he had worked) but because he had foreseen:

> . . . something else as well. The day for instance, when, if I followed in his footsteps, I would finally admit that it was all *maya*, that nothing a man could do with his life would really satisfy him, unless he were a slug and content with his own slimy wake? There were times when I almost believed Father . . . had . . . wanted to save me from discovering in too hard and too slow a way that there were no ways of matching deed to will, had wanted to put me, early on, on the quick sharp road to this discovery by getting me used to the habit of disappointment, to recognising the reality behind the apparent magic.   *Bs of P*, IV, 2

There is magic, the *maya*, the illusory world of a lost Eden, Paradise; and there is the reality, the inevitable lack of correspondence between what a man can dream and what he can encompass. Yet men are driven to dreams, to speculations on romantic possibilities, by the spirit that rules them. At the same time they are doomed to disappointment, even self-destruction, when the dreams collapse, when the possibilities are recognised as illusions, when, with Troilus in Shakespeare's bitter comedy, they recognise 'that the will is infinite, and the execution confin'd; that the desire is boundless, and the act a slave to limit'.

Many of Scott's most important concerns, then, are present in this first novel. The theatre in which they can be most fully enacted, however, is absent. Not merely is the location restricted

to a line of army encampments cut out of the Burmese jungle.
There are other attributes of fictional context that Scott needs, to
bring out the full complexity of his subject. The most conspicuous
one of these is the representation of relationships between English
and Indians. In the context of army life these relationships must
be simplified. There is no opportunity for the exploration of
private feeling between members of the two races because any
such feeling is protected and fenced in by military decorum, the
observation of rank and status. These are poor substitutes (if we
are considering the racial issue – which Scott is not, on the whole,
in *Johnnie Sahib*) for the awareness of difference of class and sex.
The only reference to the race issue as it affects relations between
men and women comes in Johnnie's treatment of the Eurasian
nurse, Nina Mackenzie; and that is both perfunctorily and not
very sensitively treated. The Eurasian issue is also touched on in
the figure of Bill Parrish's second-in-command, a man called
Johns, who pretends to come from Buckinghamshire but is in fact
the offspring of a mixed affair in India. He has never set foot in
England. Neither of these characters is made much of in *Johnnie
Sahib*. Yet the Eurasian problem, with its biological testimony to
the closest of relationships between men and women of different
races, is to figure prominently in Scott's later novels. In the *Raj
Quartet*, especially, the coming together of white and coloured in
love, hate, and (more rarely) indifference, will constitute the
fundamental *raison d'être* of the fiction. There the base on which
the whole edifice of politics, personal relationships, war and
family tradition stands, is the birth of a Eurasian child to an
English girl who has been raped by a gang of Indian youths.

THE ALIEN SKY (1953)

In Scott's second novel, *The Alien Sky*, the Eurasian subject is of
fundamental importance. The period has shifted from some time
in 1944 to June 1945, the eve of Independence. The British are
preparing to leave India, and the Cripps offer of 1942 (the right
to non-accession of some of the Muslim majority provinces) is still
fresh in the minds of members of groups within the raj. All of these
are fearful of what the future might hold for them – none more so
than the Eurasians, the despised offspring of white and coloured

men and women, who have as much to lose as anyone in the turmoil that is likely to follow the British withdrawal.

When an American businessman, Joe MacKendrick, arrives in Marapore the first British resident he speaks to is arranging to share a room at Smith's hotel with a Eurasian girl. The disclosures of this girl, Judith Anderson, to MacKendrick play an important part in the development of the plot. His next conversation, with two English women at the club, includes a good deal of gossip about half-castes, or 'chi-chis' as they are contemptuously called. Cynthia Mapleton, a plain young woman who has lost her husband in Burma and is now preparing to leave for Kenya, tells him why they are 'laughable', 'social pariahs', ridiculous in their attempts to pass themselves off as pure-bred English. 'But doesn't the colour of their skin give them away?' MacKendrick asks. And Cynthia answers: 'Not always. If it does then it turns out their mother was Spanish or something swarthy. They'll tell you anything.' What follows demonstrates the truth of Cynthia Mapleton's reply, and especially of those last four words.

For the plot of *The Alien Sky* hinges on the fact that the principal female character, Dorothy Gower, is a Eurasian. At first we do not know this, and neither do any of the characters in the novel (with one insignificant exception). Then MacKendrick learns of it from Judith Anderson, who turns out to have been a childhood friend of Dorothy's. But the fact of her mixed parentage has, in all but the literal sense (for she is white) coloured Dorothy's whole life. In particular it has destroyed what was in any case a severely strained relationship with her husband – with whom she had been forced into marriage, and who is as ignorant as everyone else about her mixed blood. He is used by her as a channel through which she can release her envy and hatred of all that is unmixed, white or brown. Until MacKendrick discovers her secret we are perplexed about her coldness towards her husband and her uncommunicativeness with everyone around her. Afterwards we understand that these things are inseparable from the strain involved in her pretensions to English birth and upbringing, the manoeuvres she has had to make to stay away from the country she has never seen and could never be at home in, and the hatred she feels towards her Indian homeland that has forced these subterfuges upon her.

Eurasian women play important roles in many of Scott's later novels, *The Chinese Love Pavilion* and *The Bender* for example. But Dorothy Gower, at the centre of this early story, is the most fully developed example of the type. And Scott has gone to a great deal of trouble to explain her predicament. For the greater part of the novel this must be by indirect means, presenting Dorothy in several difficult situations which her almost incomprehensible behaviour makes even more difficult. When Tom, her husband, tells her that he might take them back to England, she says that if he goes back there he will go without her. This strengthens his suspicion that she is having an affair with a member of the white community in Marapore, or, more likely, with John Steele, the young overseer on his farm at Ooni. MacKendrick, who overhears this conversation, also assumes that Dorothy must have a lover in India. And this encourages us to speculate on the possibility of such an affair taking place – in the light of a knowledge of her character which no one person in the novel has at his disposal. Though we meet Steele only once before Judith Anderson reveals Dorothy's secret, it becomes clear to us that it is very unlikely Dorothy is in love with him. There must be another, quite different explanation for her attitude towards her husband. When the explanation is given, much that seemed strange and even incredible about her behaviour falls into place. Her reactions to events are seen to have been determined by something which makes them psychologically plausible, as well as dramatically enigmatic.

Dorothy Gower's dilemma might have emerged more clearly as the subject of the novel if it had not been obscured by the interference in her life of the American, MacKendrick. He too has a humiliating secret, which drives him to force his attentions on to Dorothy long before he becomes aware of the circumstances of her birth. MacKendrick has come to Marapore to lay a private ghost. He feels he has to overcome certain deficiencies in his character which have been created by a bullying and sadistic brother. Again we are introduced to a subject that was absent from *Johnnie Sahib*, but which is to play a very large part in the later novels: the perverse, often sadistic relationships which can develop between elder and younger brothers. Sometimes the blood-relationship between the two men is not so close, and in the most deeply explored example – Ronald Merrick's relationship with Hari Kumar in the *Raj Quartet* – it is absent altogether. Scott shows no interest in any complementary relationship between sisters: Sarah and Susan Layton, for example, behave towards each other in a quite different way. Incidentally, Scott's decision to make his principal 'half-caste' character in the *Quartet* a young man (Hari Kumar) rather than a young woman, is without precedent in the earlier novels, and in any case his half-caste identity is a cultural rather than a genetic phenomenon. In his next novel, *A Male Child*, the fraternal relationship is at the centre of the plot. It is almost equally important in *The Mark of the Warrior* and *The Corrida at San Felíu*. In *The Bender* it is looked at from the other side of the relationship, from the point of view of the elder rather than the younger brother.

In *The Alien Sky*, Joe's brother Dwight has recently died in the war in the Pacific. MacKendrick's interest in Dorothy is awakened by this fact, for in the process of sorting out his brother's possessions he has found a pile of letters Dorothy wrote to Dwight, pleading with him not to abandon her to her unsatisfactory marriage with Tom Gower. He has also left a letter of his own, written to Dorothy but never sent to her, which contains a puzzling sentence to the effect that 'what you told me that time *would* make a difference'. The puzzle is solved, of course, when we discover that she was referring to her mixed blood, which she had confessed to Dwight. Before that, MacKendrick had assumed Dorothy meant she couldn't have children (which in a sense was true, because they might have been brown children). In any case he sees Dwight's treatment of Dorothy as typical of his ruthlessness and cruelty, frequently inflicted on himself when they were young boys, and determines to free himself from his demoralising attachment to his dead brother by taking his discarded mistress from him. But now that he has discovered the real reason for Dwight's treatment of Dorothy, his attitude towards her becomes more complicated. So does his relationship with her husband, now that he can correctly interpret Dorothy's ill-treatment of him as a hideously unjust retribution on the whole white male sex – of which Tom, with his unpopular liberal sentiments, is such an unrepresentative example.

The problem that arises from this aspect of the plotting has to do with the representation of MacKendrick's motives *before* he hears the truth about Dorothy. What is he trying to achieve by forming an attachment with his dead brother's mistress? How does he suppose this will lift the burden of his subjection to Dwight, his sense of inferiority to Dwight, from his shoulders? What sort of relationship does he have in mind, in any case? Is it a protective affection, a more satisfactory answer to her love-letters than the deceitful and callous response his brother was preparing to make? Or has he in mind a cynically sexual liaison in which he will make use of her much as Dwight made use of her, thus lowering himself to his brother's moral level – so brilliantly successful within its own terms of reference? There is too much confusion about this matter for us to enter into MacKendrick's feelings sympathetically. They remain a blur close to the centre of the novel, and the blur obscures much of Dorothy as well as her would-be lover. Perhaps Scott is trying to achieve too much here, prematurely introducing two of his abiding obsessions, and forcing them into unconvincing relationship with each other. His next novel, *A Male Child*, will concentrate on the theme of sibling relationships in an altogether different context, where other complex family relationships provide a more appropriate background. In *The Alien Sky* we feel the obsession intrudes awkwardly on the other, more comprehensible obsession with racial identity and miscegenation.

Certainly the most powerfully moving scenes in this novel have to do with the treatment of Eurasians by members of the white community. The first of these describes a party at which Judith's pretensions to having been brought up in Brighton are cruelly exposed by Cynthia Mapleton – an event which is responsible for her confession about Dorothy to MacKendrick. The second is at the end of the book when MacKendrick, about to make love to Dorothy, accuses her of deceiving Gower for inadequate and totally sadistic reasons:

> You could have told him what you were long ago, couldn't you? You've deliberately not told him because all you wanted him to feel was how much you hated him . . . What happens now? How long do you intend to hate me? That's how its going to be isn't it? Having your own back on me because of Dwight. Having your own back on Tom because you were forced to marry him. They're both the same. What happens when

you've got nobody left to get your own back on? What happens
when you've got nobody left to hate?

The predictable answer is returned:

There'll be myself, won't there? That's what you want me to
say! That there'll be myself!   *The Alien Sky*, III, 2

The scene is not melodramatic because it issues out of a fatally
plausible conjunction of two people at a stage in their lives when
they feel driven to hurt and be revenged on a world that has
humiliated them. So when MacKendrick enters her, she makes
an animal response. He is driven to impotence and she dismisses
him with scorn. He claims she was thinking of Dwight. She
attributes her refusal to be possessed to her habit of withholding
herself. And it is a fact that she withholds the truth about herself
from Tom Gower on a physical level, as well as on the level of her
'genetic' identity: 'There's always been part of me he hasn't
knowingly possessed . . . If he knew what I was I'd have nothing
left to withhold.'
     The episode is a very painful dramatisation of the connection
in Dorothy's mind between her racial secret, her social frigidity
and her manipulation of her sex to humiliate others. The fact that
MacKendrick is the victim upon whom she inflicts this humiliation is suffused with a most brutal irony. After all, his original
attitude towards her was also based on a need to punish others
and satisfy his injured pride; though, as I have suggested, *how*
these needs were to be satisfied remains a mystery, because the
connection between sexual desire and punishment is unclear. But
now that he has discovered Dorothy's secret, both she and her
husband have ceased to be mere 'images'. They are 'people who
exist outside you and in spite of you. You may know the image
backwards but you don't know what's behind it or within it. You
don't know *her* in the way you knew Dwight. You've set an image
against a man and you've judged.' Now that kind of judgement is
turned against him as Dorothy fails to see in him also anything
more than 'an image'. At the moment he tries to get beyond his
previous role as Dwight's substitute, Dorothy sees him and
Dwight and Tom as indistinguishable representatives of the
despised white male sex, and herself as the white girl who won't

play 'chi-chi'. She withholds herself at the point where her sex and her mixed blood run together and stagnate.

Tom Gower has to be understood throughout as the unknowing victim of Dorothy's Eurasian conscience. Her frigidity, her infidelity, her mysterious changes of mind about whether or not she will go to England or whether she will go to Kalipur (the Princely State in which the Maharajah has invited Tom to become an adviser) are all entangled with Gower's eviction from his farm and removal from his position on the newspaper he edits. Unlike MacKendrick or Dorothy, Gower contrived to live in a kind of Paradise, one that bound him deeply to an India that seems no longer to want him. On the one hand he has to accept that he has fifteen years of self-deception standing between himself and reality; on the other that, deception or otherwise, this is his world, 'and a man and his world are inseparable'. Tragically, on a merely physical level, the reality of his connection with India is in Dorothy. Her mixed blood is the physical equivalent of his mixed relationship with the world from which he cannot separate himself. But history and social mores and Dorothy's own attitude to these things (as well as her physical dislike) have removed this consolation from him. The book ends with his unsuccessful attempt at suicide and Dorothy's unloving return to their house in Marapore: ' "I've come back here," ' she said at last. ' "And Tom will come back too, I suppose." '

A MALE CHILD (1956)

A minor character, John Steele, who was Gower's assistant on his farm at Ooni, reappears casually in a conversation between two of the main characters of Scott's next book, *A Male Child*. This is the first sign of a habit that will begin to exert profound changes on the structure of the novels immediately preceding the *Raj Quartet*. In the *Quartet* itself, references are made occasionally to characters in the earlier novels: e.g. Robert Conway, of *The Birds of Paradise*, is adviser to the Nawab of Gopalakand, with whom Nigel Rowan is negotiating off-stage in *A Division of the Spoils*.

A Male Child itself lies somewhat to the side of Scott's

development, though aspects of the book suggest he may be exploring areas of direct personal experience. Many of these are superficial: the setting in Pelham (not Palmers) Green; one of the two principal characters' training in accountancy. The preoccupation with relationships between elder and younger brothers, on the model of what we have already discovered in *The Alien Sky*, might be a more basic matter. It is not altogether easy to dispel the impression that in spite of the kind of first-person narrative in which it is written (which has nothing in common with the conventional first-person *confessional* style) much of the substance of this novel is autobiographical. Certainly it leaves the impression of being one of the most secretive of Scott's books, skating over depths of private obsession that remain for the most part inscrutable and mysterious.

One of the reasons for this, I think, is the central position occupied by what might be called the substitution theme. Over and over again in Scott's fiction we discover one of the characters, sometimes deliberately, sometimes quite innocently, displacing another by occupying what he believes is his rightful position in the novel's scheme of things. Sometimes the occupation is physical: one of the characters actually takes over the position another has been used to filling. At other times it is a psychological occupation: a place in one of the characters' thoughts and feelings about the world, that has in the past been settled by one person, is usurped by another. Modifications introduced into a situation by one or other of these two kinds of occupation account for some of the most startling effects produced by the novels.

In *A Male Child* this fact is more remarkable than usual, because the central web of relationships is one in which both kinds of substitution have taken place. In a physical sense Alan Hurst has been thrust into the centre of his family's affairs after his older brother, Edward, has been killed in the war. But his mother cannot accept that Edward is dead. She sees his ghost haunting the family house at Aylward. Later she detects in Alan's friend Ian Canning, the narrator of the story, a person so uncannily like Edward that he appears in her eyes almost as if he *were* her elder son. The physical likeness is remarked on by other characters. At different times Adela Coles (Alan's older cousin), Mrs Voremberg (a neighbour), and Alan himself comment on the resemblance – though none of them finds it as striking as Mrs Hurst does.

What Mrs Voremberg says about the two men draws attention to certain peculiarities in Canning's resemblance to Edward, suggesting that Alan's mother's identification of the one with the other is more than fanciful. We have to bear in mind that Mrs Voremberg is a crank, battening on the severe depression Mrs Hurst has experienced after the loss of her son. Nevertheless she really does seem to believe that Edward has been in the house ever since his death; and that she has freed his mother from his presence by willing him down to her room and keeping him there. The only occasions on which Edward (or his ghost) has left her room were when Alan's wife, Stella, came to live there; and when Ian Canning arrived – since which time he has never returned. There is a rumour that Stella had always loved Edward more than she loved his brother, which would explain his ghostly release to her and her subsequent separation from Alan. Canning's arrival in the house at the precise moment when Mrs Voremberg sensed Edward's disappearance from her room (which was also the moment when Mrs Hurst first mistook him for her elder son) substantiates the claim the book seems to be making that Ian really is, in some sense, a tangible substitute for Edward in the lives of those who have been closest to him.

In spite of his physical frailty, Ian's arrival at Aylward is made to look like what Edward's arrival there would have been if he had survived the war. Although he does not wish to supplant Alan in his mother's and his fiancée's affections, he is made to appear to do so by the exigencies of the plot. And since Alan is responsible for much of the early development of the plot, it seems at times that he is almost deliberately withdrawing into the background, taking upon himself the status of the passive, dominated younger brother. There is no more fitting explanation of his bringing Ian to the house and arranging to have thrust upon him many of Edward's duties and even, in respect of Stella, his affections.

But Ian's connection with Edward operates at a deeper level than this. He himself senses the presence of Alan's dead brother in the house. When he enters the house, Mrs Hurst will not allow him to sleep in Edward's old room. After meeting him, however, and talking with him about Edward and the rest of the family, she offers him the room and he settles into it almost as another Edward might have done. One of Edward's pictures on the wall, a reproduction of Sickert's *L'Ennui*, is familiar. At first Ian supposes it is a picture he too had once possessed. Then he realises that it belonged to his wife, Helena, from whom he is separated (a situation which brings him closer to Alan than to Edward). Later, when Stella returns to Aylward, pregnant with Alan's child, Ian accompanies her to the clinic, just as Edward might have done if he had survived or if he himself had married her. At this point Ian's estrangement from Helena and Alan's neglect of his wife precipitates Ian into a 'married' relationship with Stella which is a ghostly projection of old Mrs Hurst's ambitions for her favourite son. In his relations with Mrs Hurst, too, Ian takes over Edward's role when he accepts responsibility for curing her of her alcoholism. Receiving the bottle she must be allowed only at irregular and infrequent intervals, he says that he saw the expression on Alan's face and 'I realised the choice I had made disturbed him. There was no going back on it, though; and no escape from the knowledge that, as Edward had always done, I had pushed him into the background.'

The real bond between Ian and Edward, apart from their similarities of physique and temperament, is their closeness to death. Edward has already crossed the boundary between life and death, though he has left a part of himself behind to haunt the living. Ian is preparing for death, either by suicide or by the slow, intermittent progress in him of a tropical disease he contracted during war service in the Far East. When Mrs Hurst first saw Ian on the landing at Aylward she mistook him for Edward, and even when she had seen her mistake she made a mental comparison between him and her son: 'I thought this other thing about you, that you had decided to have no future. You had Edward's look of that last leave when he went away and I knew he knew he was going to die.' The suggestion is that Ian's substitution for Edward in the lives of the household originates as much in his closeness to Edward's condition (of death) as it does in the uses to which he can be put, the roles he can be made to perform (as Edward's *alter ego*) in their lives. Ian feels this most strongly, and most intimately, when he experiences his first bout of fever at Aylward. He is in Edward's bedroom at the time. As he struggles to open the upper portion of the window above his bed, then contemplates the alternative of throwing himself out into the darkness, he feels Edward's presence. Indeed he says he '*knew*, without any doubt whatsoever, that Edward was there':

> There was nothing unpleasant or frightening about it. I did not see him, but unmistakably he was there, quite close to me, the whole of him making itself known in a resigned exhalation of breath which I heard, and felt upon my cheek; and there was something so melancholy about it that I was filled with an overwhelming sense of loss.   *A Male Child*, 1, 6

As the fever abates, Ian feels himself 'withdrawing himself from it, withdrawing myself from death and from Edward'.

Partly Canning's assumption of the role of Edward's ghost is a vivid metaphorical representation of his own sickness and his own inclination towards death; partly it is a response to the needs of the people around him; and partly it is a way of bringing into clearer focus the actual relationship between Alan and Edward when they were both alive. Ian's behaviour towards Mrs Hurst and Stella and Adela Coles mirrors the behaviour of Edward, only a few years ago, to those same people. The identification of Ian with Edward is broken when Stella returns to Aylward and bears Alan a male child. Now Mrs Hurst has a new elder 'son' on whom she will be able to impose Edward's image; and Ian, we assume, leaves Aylward to resume a life of sorts elsewhere.

Not all of *A Male Child* is written with the same intensity as the scenes in Edward's room and the conversations between Ian Canning and Mrs Hurst there. The narrative tends to flatness and drift, even though the organisation of the plot is cleverly contrived to emphasise the ambiguous role Canning is called upon to play. The depths of the book, however, are locked away in Canning's mind. They are incapable of declaring themselves fully in the dialogue and the external action. An obsessive psychology is allowed to unfold within a peculiarly appropriate framework of plot. But the correspondence between the psychology of the characters and the plot is not always brought home as forcefully as it needs to be in the detail of the narrative. Scott is to make more subtle and more consistently powerful use of this device of substitution later, in *The Birds of Paradise*, *The Corrida at San Felíu* and, most brilliantly of all, in the *Quartet*. There it becomes a remarkably subtle method of linking narratives at a level far beneath the crude patternings of the plot. In *A Male Child*, though, the substitution *is* the plot. That says something about the relatively simple manipulation of narrative of which Scott was capable during the period when he wrote this novel.

THE MARK OF THE WARRIOR (1958)

After 1960 Paul Scott resigned his position as director of the publishing company with which he had been associated for many years, and became a full-time professional writer. The change of life corresponded with a sudden development of his technical resources – only slightly evident in *The Chinese Love Pavilion*, which he published in 1960, but immensely assured in *The Birds of Paradise* of 1962. The first of these novels I should judge to be one of Scott's most ambitious but least successful pieces. He is evidently trying to communicate a vision of life which he is not yet capable of articulating either in the terms of his previous narrative style, or in the evolving symbolic structures which were to follow. For this reason I prefer the last of the novels which belong to the first stage of his writing career (*The Mark of the Warrior*) to the first of the later, denser and more difficult novels (which is what I take *The Chinese Love Pavilion* to be).

Scott has not written a more carefully constructed and unblemished narrative than he did in this, his fourth novel. The cast is small. The action is clearly focused and free from distracting minor incidents. The writing has a tautness, a thrusting efficiency both in dialogue and description, which occasionally gives way to something else: a more richly poetic style, describing the jungle landscape, and drawing attention to aspects of the human mind and spirit which find in that landscape their unconscious analogue. The jungle with its two conspicuous features – the forest and the river – is the setting of most of this novel. But it is more than this. It is the testing ground of the characters' imagination and military resourcefulness, a challenge to them to reveal whether they do or do not possess what Scott has called 'the mark of the warrior'.

The action begins in the jungle. In a brief Prologue we are introduced to a column of soldiers, the remnants of an Indian rifle company, crossing a river in the hills of Upper Burma. The battalion has been attacked by Japanese four days ago, and is now heading towards Imphal. When the crossing is half completed, the raft that has been contructed to carry provisions and help the non-swimmers across disintegrates. At the same time the men are attacked by a small enemy patrol. Five men are drowned, two desert into the jungle, and three are shot dead. One of the men who die is John Ramsay, the only white officer in the group. The commander, Major Craig, buries him and moves on, arriving in India two weeks later with what remains of his company.

This brief incident, the only direct account of a military engagement in the whole of Scott's work (there is an *indirect* account of another small incident in *The Day of the Scorpion*) contains the seeds of everything that follows. Craig's life is dominated by his failure, as he sees it, to have avoided the catastrophe described in the Prologue. His fear of the jungle springs from his fear of his own inadequacy as a soldier and as a leader of men. Ramsay is dead: his response to the jungle can be inferred only from what the Major says and thinks about him. His place in the moral scheme of the book is taken by his younger brother, Bob, who has turned up at the Officers' Training School Craig is running, a day and a half's railway journey North East of Poona. (It is now January 1943, six months or so after the disaster.)

The plot of the novel is arranged so as to bring Craig and young Ramsay into almost exactly the same situation as the one in which Craig and John Ramsay were placed in the Prologue. The differences are significant; but not so significant as to obscure how what happens here, at the end of the novel, helps to explain what happened there, in the Prologue, almost a year before. The way the incident arises, and the attitudes the two men adopt towards it, defines their characters – as the Argument of the novel seeks to define character. 'Three things are to be considered', it says: 'a man's estimate of himself, the face he presents to the world, the estimate of that man made by other men. Combined, they form an aspect of truth.' By the end of the novel all of these three things have been considered in relation to Craig and Ramsay. An aspect of truth has been defined. Unsurprisingly, however, in view of the rest of Scott's work, the way things fall out makes it clear that 'an aspect of truth' is different from 'the truth' itself. Always there are complications that suggest the ambiguous nature of human behaviour, especially when viewed in its moral aspect.

The most obvious difference between the two events is that one of them is 'real' – an actual incident experienced by Craig and Ramsay in their flight from the Japanese; and the other is simulated – part of a military exercise conducted by Craig and his sergeant-major (Thompson) only thirty miles away from the Training School. But for Craig and young Ramsay the difference is only superficial. Since the escape to Imphal, Craig has never ventured into the jungle. When he has to do so for the first time, to check on the site of the war game, the reality of the challenge to his self-respect, and, beneath that, his self-image, is undeniable.

The way the challenge presents itself is outwardly trivial. Near the centre of the site, a section of river beneath a spur of rock he names Elephant Hill, Craig insists on leaving his wife alone with Thompson so that he can check the river crossing deeper into the forest. After near-panic at being lost in the forest he finds his way back. On his approach he sees that Esther is where he left her and is already safe, although oblivious of his presence behind her. Thompson is apart from them, down by the river bed. His expression when he turns round makes it clear that he knew Craig was there. This picture of Esther and Thompson, apart both physically and in their awareness or unawareness of what is happening in the jungle, crystallises in Craig's mind the difference between himself and not only Thompson, but the two Ramsays as well: 'When he looked round I saw that he was alone in the forest and wanted to be alone in the forest because he was in the forest *to kill*.' He smiles, and adds, 'Whereas I, and most of the men I remember, were in the forest to live . . . Except John Ramsay. He was in the forest in Thompson's way. It's like a mark on them.'

The subtlety of the situation lies in the fact that in order to live in the forest, people like Craig need people like Thompson and Ramsay. Without them they would not survive. So they have to find a man, or create one, whose urge to destroy and kill will protect them from being destroyed and killed in their turn. This is a terrible responsibility. *How* terrible will depend on the extent to which the required qualities of single-mindedness and savagery

are already dormant in the man who is chosen, or have to be
created in him – against his own nature. When Craig identifies
young Ramsay as someone who, like his brother, can be trained
to become such a man, his conscience is appalled. That he does
make the identification, and acts upon it, is at the heart of the
double tragedy Scott has made the subject of his book.

Young Ramsay discovers the site on an unauthorised sortie
into the jungle. Then he is given the responsibility of leading his
fellow-cadets on the mock assault which is to follow. The way
Craig meets Ramsay on his way to Elephant Hill is symptomatic
of what is to come. It tells us a great deal about Ramsay's
preparedness for the role that is being thrust on him. Craig
cannot be said to find Ramsay, in spite of the fact that he is a
senior officer tracking down a cadet who is out of bounds. Instead
Ramsay finds Craig, sensing his presence in the forest with an
almost animal instinct. In the military manoeuvres that are to
follow, this instinct will acquire a high moral value because of its
usefulness, its peculiar adaptability to circumstances of conflict
and warfare:

> He could not be sure, afterwards, whether he had heard some
> small sound of movement down to his right. When he thought
> about it, at other times, it seemed as though that is what must
> have happened. But then, standing alone and waiting for some
> sign, he suffered a muffling of senses of the left side of his body
> and a sharpening of those on the right, so that he turned in that
> direction and went cautiously down the slope. And now both
> to the right and the left he experienced that curious muffling of
> sound, a muffling on either side of a channel of clarity which
> led him with certainty forward in the direction of the river. So
> strange was this sensation that at first he was afraid, but when
> it persisted he understood its purpose and then he was not
> afraid but excited in a new way; excited not at the intimation
> of power, but with the power itself as he felt it clothe him in
> invulnerability.   *The Mark of the Warrior*, 1, 'Ramsay' 5

The second part of the novel describes the war game Craig and
Ramsay have already prepared. It demonstrates Ramsay's
qualities of leadership. And it emphasises Craig's uncertain
control over the situation he has helped to establish, and over his

own attitude to the object of the exercise. Also, by introducing a new character, Blake, who commands the opposing forces in the game, it defines more starkly than would have been possible otherwise the strengths and weaknesses of the 'warrior' Ramsay is discovering himself to be.

For Blake the whole exercise is something of a joke, a mere game. He is prepared to play fast and loose with the element of pretence in it. Trucks ferrying supplies to the two camps along jungle roads are substitutes for light aircraft dropping supplies from overhead. Blake interferes with this ground supply system, strictly against the rules. By doing so he discloses his inability to involve himself seriously in the artificial situation each of the contestants is supposed to imagine is real. Ramsay's attitude to the exercise is diametrically opposite. 'Above all', he says, 'I want to establish reality.' When Blake has played his trick with the supply trucks, and has sent out a spy (called Baksh) to ascertain the direction in which they are moving, Ramsay feels he has to incorporate the trick as a new element in the 'real' situation. He makes use of the spy (whose presence therefore has to be accounted for according to a different hypothesis – consistent with the other terms of reference of the exercise) in his assault on Blake's troops. When Craig explains the situation that has been created by Baksh's presence in Ramsay's camp, Blake fails to understand the nature of the change. As Craig tells him, he is looking at it all wrong: 'You're looking at it from the point of view of officer-cadet Ramsay conducting an exercise and dependent from time to time on ration trucks from the school. Can't you for once be what you're supposed to be and treat Ramsay as what he's supposed to be? . . .' Even Craig fails to understand fully the reality of the situation Ramsay has created. On one occasion, when Ramsay has been speaking to the men about Blake and Baksh in a way calculated to involve them deeply in what is happening, Craig interrupts with a point of order. Ramsay is obviously angry with him because he has 'broken the spell' he had been weaving. Through Craig's words they had come back from the illusion into the exercise. Craig appreciates Ramsay's point of view. In his later talk with Blake he says: 'What we're doing, the purpose of what we're doing, is real to me . . . And there are certain things which are real in any case.' In other words, as the feelings of the men and the patterns of their manoeuvres develop and grow more complicated, the line that divides an exercise from a real manoeuvre blurs and disappears. Ramsay imposes a reality on the situation from which, eventually, no one will be able to escape.

Like Part I, Part II is written in chapters which contain descriptions of events as they are experienced alternately by Craig and by Ramsay. But the purpose of this division is clearer than it was before. Ramsay is growing further away from the 'official' military point of view represented by Craig, as he becomes more self-sufficient, more dependent on the men he controls than on the commanding officer who had sought to control him. What Craig sees, however, is different in another sense from what Ramsay sees. What Craig sees is the efflorescence of the warrior ethic in Ramsay, which he had sought to persuade him to recognise but which, when recognition has come, takes Ramsay far beyond Craig's comprehension. What Ramsay sees is the not altogether expected, and certainly quite novel development of his own capacity for leadership. What he experiences is the mystique of command. This means that each man's understanding of the other is conveyed in different terms from the way it was conveyed in the first Part. There, Craig had the advantage over Ramsay – though the damage his earlier experiences had inflicted on his self-confidence rendered the advantage something of a hollow one. Here Ramsay has the advantage over Craig, as his own experience of jungle warfare, though 'unreal' in the obvious sense of that word, tells him more and more about the reasons for Craig's self-distrust.

The main subject of the two men's speculations is the question of how John Ramsay died. The circumstances of the death are unclear to everyone except Craig. (No one knows whether or not Craig shot him to put him out of his agony, after he was seriously wounded by Japanese sniper fire.) The reasons for it are unclear even to him. It is only when Ramsay questions him more and more searchingly about what happened in the jungle a year ago that the Major realises what might have lain behind John Ramsay's conduct, before the raft collapsed and he was killed.

Craig had always supposed that Ramsay's death was his fault, because he was the CO, and in the last resort the men rely on their CO. But Bob Ramsay's experience at the ford during the exercise at Elephant Mountain teaches him that his brother must have 'bodged the raft on purpose', so as to secure the crossing and at the same time rid the company of the weak links (the non-swimmers) in the chain of command. In Bob Ramsay's view, though, the fact remains that his brother should not have been in the position in which Craig placed him: the nucleus of the whole unit, feeling himself to be responsible for the men and the pattern of interlinked activity they represented. Craig's failure had been to allow John Ramsay to accept this burden, when he recognised that his own responsiveness to the jungle was less acute than that of his subordinate officer. Since John accepted that responsibility, however, he had broken a sacred trust by sacrificing the men on the raft. Craig's decision about what to do with him after he was wounded by the Japanese, therefore, was mistaken. Craig had waited for him to die, in great pain, rather than finish him off (as John had wished). Ramsay would have shot him. To Craig's question 'Why? Because he'd murdered the men who drowned?', Ramsay replies: 'No. Because he'd murdered himself. He couldn't face up to the weak links. He broke the pattern deliberately. He broke his own image.' It is clear from this exchange, almost at the end of the novel, that Ramsay has become, completely, the instrument Craig had guiltily attempted to forge. His brother has become an example of a failed warrior. He himself has become one dominant and controlling unit that has lost its human identity as a result of the position it occupies in a total pattern of activity.

Ramsay's understanding of his own role as a leader first emerges half-way through the exercise in the jungle, after he has explained to Craig what he intends to do about Baksh. Craig is taken aback, telling him: 'You make it all sound very mechanical, as if people weren't involved at all.' There is some truth in this. But Craig doesn't begin to understand Ramsay's state of mind:

> He began his tour of the perimeter, and as he went pride grew within a sense of corporate safety because his world, his circle of land, was awake, alert, sensitive. A kind of love, an excitement at the pattern his will had imposed upon the ground, moved him, hardened him. He felt immensely powerful, the sum of all of them, the whole of which they were only parts.   *The Mark of the Warrior*, II, 'Ramsay' 2

During the assault both Craig and the cadets are thankful for Ramsay's gifts as they deliver themselves 'into the hands of the whole man who was not for them a man at all but the sum of their separate longings to survive in the dark, green, drowned world'. They accept the positions they must occupy in the pattern Ramsay has contrived to defeat the enemy. 'Pattern' is a word he makes use of frequently in his self-communings. He means by it the subjection of his own personality to the interests of the whole company. By now that personality is one that has learned to know itself more fully in the heart of the jungle. It has become more itself than it ever was before. Nevertheless it is willingly sacrificed in the interest of the larger unit: 'The pattern which I lay down on the ground in front of the men are the patterns of my own body . . . Here, where I stand, is the heart of the pattern.' Ramsay goes on to describe the interlocking of his and Blake's patterns: 'I have become a pattern which moves through the forest to attack another pattern, and in the struggle between pattern and pattern is the shape of the struggle between myself and this other man, between myself and Blake.'

When Ramsay confesses 'I am one hundred men . . . but I am not in myself a man', he suggests the extent and the limitations of his power. 'I am one hundred links in a chain which is only the image of a chain. I must preserve the image of the chain. If the image is destroyed I am also destroyed. I am nothing without the image and the image is nothing without me.' The strain, as well as the elation, of maintaining this view of the self is made vividly apparent in those passages which emphasise the opposite scale on the dynamic balance of Ramsay's sensibility: that is to say, those passages of personal communion where the urge to cut oneself away from the pattern that is no pattern without the man who controls it is felt very strongly. Another metaphor Ramsay uses to describe this deep longing for separation, and the coming into full personal identity which he believes will result from it, is that of the nerves being severed from the centre. Then the centre will 'go back into myself so that I might be alone in the forest and move in my own safety towards an end or a beginning of my own making'. The emphasis on what is 'my own', and the powerful regressive direction of these sentiments, suggest a feeling of intense privacy which is the reverse of the complete anonymity, the subjection of the self to the pattern, that being a warrior must entail. It is a state of mind explored more fully, but equally bafflingly, I think, in the portrait of Brian Saxby in *The Chinese Love Pavilion*.

'It is what I am forced to be, but wish not to be.' That is Ramsay's understanding of his predicament before the fording of the river and the assault on Blake. It explains Craig's predicament also, in judging the point at which he is bringing out qualities in a man which are latent in him, and where he is imposing on him a warrior-identity that is not the natural expression of his character. As he puts it to himself in Khudabad, when Ramsay has left for the forest:

> I create Ramsay in the image of the man I should have been perhaps, but could not be: the image of a man who feels the need to destroy his enemies, who finds this need greater than his own need to live, who therefore mocks his life.
>
> Almost without knowing Craig moved towards the forest. I'm wrong, he thought, I do not create Ramsay in this image. It is the image in which he is cast and I take his hand and move the fingers across his brow so that he may feel grown there indelibly into the flesh the stamp, the mark of the warrior, and when he has felt this mark and understood its nature he will be a man into whose hands the rest of us may place our lives.
>
> *The Mark of the Warrior*, ii, 'Craig' 4

Craig is not mistaken in Ramsay. He did genuinely feel 'the mark of the warrior' stamped indelibly into the flesh. But he seems to have no knowledge of the extra cost, the denial of the new privacy the forest has provided. Ramsay was drowned not by trying to save somebody else, but himself. By 'himself', Craig means the image of what he had become; what Craig, as he supposes, had made him. Now he regrets this. He had thought he was helping him 'to be what I thought he had it in him to be, but he had other things in him as well and I let him destroy them.' Craig's assessment of Ramsay is debatable. It is probably more applicable to John Ramsay than to the younger brother, who seems to have discovered in himself just such a warrior as Craig had hoped to find. But what Craig neglects altogether, and what makes the actual moment of Ramsay's death so different from anything Craig can imagine, is the presence of that 'world he had looked for and which, at the end, he knew no man could enter until the end'. This is something the forest has taught him – as the forest is to teach it, in some strange sense, to Brian Saxby, in Malaya, two years later.

Saxby, though, is mad – or becomes so, living with his strange knowledge. Perhaps *The Mark of the Warrior* is all the more effective as a novel for killing off Ramsay before he can be made to articulate what Saxby is made to articulate in *The Chinese Love Pavilion*. We have felt his experience of the forest very powerfully, and seen how it can be converted, with advantages of a kind, to effective military purposes. The metaphysical character of the experience is left in abeyance. It must be said that there is no obvious way in which one can imagine its presence would have strengthened this novel. Or so the record of what was to follow strongly suggests.

In novels like *The Chinese Love Pavilion*, *The Birds of Paradise*, and *The Corrida at San Felíu* Scott was to evolve a much more complex handling of narrative than the one he had deployed in *Johnnie Sahib* or *The Mark of the Warrior*. There he had relied on the direct representation of events in temporal sequence, incorporating the occasional flashback or abrupt change of scene. But he had done little to extend these techniques to produce a multi-layered effect of narrative superimposed on narrative, episode cutting into episode, and the whole tentatively organising itself around what is gradually discovered to be the central pivot of the novel's structure. In other words he had learnt little from what had been so important a strategy in the novels of Conrad – whose example I have already suggested had great deal to do with Scott's preoccupations, as well as techniques, as a writer.

After *The Mark of the Warrior*, a transformation of narrative into something densely suggestive of the mysteries and uncertainties attending the fates of men becomes more prominent. Scott begins to exercise control over the plots of his novels by arranging them in poetic rather than in merely sequential patterns. The narrative sequence doesn't break down altogether, but it tends to be dissolved and reorganised by a mind intent on reminiscence, or exploration, or even creative fabrication deriving from the 'real' events that lie, inert and futile, behind the complex pattern of the novel. *The Corrida at San Felíu* offers the most extreme example of this sort of temporal dislocation. As I shall argue at the appropriate time, it is much to Paul Scott's credit in writing the *Corrida* that he was able to interweave such a complicated sequence of episodes in the interests of psychological clarity rather than the merely technical obfuscation which has so often been the result of this kind of experiment.

3 Towards the *Quartet*

There are two kinds of people in the world: those who are
embattled in strong citadels which are strong however unjustly
or foolishly they are administered, and those who go out like
gaunt Don Quixotes on ribby horses to tilt at bulls or the
monotonous grinding sails of windmills.

The Corrida at San Felíu, Part Two, 2

He was a man who understood the oddity, the eccentricity of
life, and he would always respond to whatever it was in a
situation that promised to make it greater than its
circumstances.

The Chinese Love Pavilion, ii, i

A man that is born falls into a dream like a man who falls into
the sea. If he tries to climb out into the air as inexperienced
people endeavour to do, he drowns – *nicht wahr?* . . . No! I tell
you! The way is to the destructive element submit yourself, and
with the exertions of your hands and feet in the water make the
deep, deep sea keep you up.

Conrad, *Lord Jim*, Chapter 20

THE CHINESE LOVE PAVILION (1960)

For the most part the common narrative conventions are
observed in *The Chinese Love Pavilion*. The Prologue, however –
'The door by which men enter' – powerfully involves us in a
description of the love pavilion and its grounds which, in spite of
the title, appears to have little to do with the narrative that
follows. We have to wait another hundred pages before we

discover where the pavilion is, in what circumstances the things that were said in it were said, and the significance of Tom Brent's gift of a Malayan *kris* to Teena Chang. The first sentence of the first chapter rather surprisingly opens with the words: 'The story begins not with Teena Chang but with a man called Brian Saxby, and it begins before the war in India, not in Malaya.'

What immediately follows is a quite interesting and straightforwardly told story in the first person of Brent's early adventures in India. But it is not at all in the style of the Prologue, with its suggestive topography of the place of execution in the garden of madness, the merchant's house 'in the Eurasian style' behind it, and the orientally-designed pavilion on the other side where the tiles of the roof, once painted in gold, still glow above the dragon posts. This description is a foretaste of descriptions in the *Quartet* – of the MacGregor House and the Bibighar gardens, with their history of the house of the singer and the house of the courtesans, and the ghosts that flit between them. With the *Quartet* behind us we should expect to see enacted at the scene some pale analogy of the past transposed into modern terms and subject to contemporary consequences and judgements – the same is to be true of the legend of the island on Krishi's estate at Jundapur in *The Birds of Paradise*, where William, Dora and Krishi enact the story of Krishna, the princess and the princess's brother.

Inside the pavilion we are introduced to the three rooms (Golden, Jade and Scarlet) and the unnamed anteroom whose twin doors are christened by Teena and Brent 'the door by which men enter in anticipation of desire' and 'the door by which men go in memory of loving'. So mysterious and poetically suggestive are these opening pages about the pavilion that we are not surprised to find the building interpreted by Brent as an emblem of the human heart:

> And the heart was, in its complexity, as strange and mysterious as the pavilion with its chambers of different colours, its doors to come in by and to go out of, its strong supporting pillars awrithe with dragons. But within it there was always the illusion of the occasion found. *The Chinese Love Pavilion*, II, 7

These last words are very important. They identify the pavilion with a kind of paradise, an exotic edifice separated from the military cantonment and the merchants' houses on either side, and impregnated by a mysterious lovemaking. Here the identities of the ordinary, often callow young soldiers are transformed by the silken robes they wear before they enter. On one level the pavilion is the very emblem of the heart's illusion of Paradise, 'the illusion of the occasion found'. On another it is a high-class bawdy-house presided over by an experienced prostitute who may have collaborated with the Japanese. It is erected near the place of their executions in the garden of madness. And it is the site of the death of the beautiful Lieutenant Hakinawa – long before his English successor, Brent, came upon the scene. Certainly the establishment of the pavilion as a leitmotif, so early in the novel, introduces a mysterious factor into a story which only gradually moves towards it as a part of the geography of the narrative. This occurs only after many other, apparently disconnected, episodes have overlain it in our thoughts.

The main strand of narrative in *The Chinese Love Pavilion* is less concerned with Teena Chang and the pavilion than with Tom Brent's attempt to track down Brian Saxby in the jungles of Malaya. Before the war Saxby had persuaded Brent to stay in India and confront his destiny. The means by which he did this are interesting in so far as they suggest Conradian preoccupations, modified in the light of sixty years of history. For the terms in which Saxby addresses Brent at this important stage in his fortunes are those that Stein used in his conversation with Jim in Chapter 20 of Conrad's novel. Saxby asks Brent if he has read Conrad:

'No.'

'He was a Pole who wrote in English . . . He said that directly a man is born he's flung into his dream as if into a sea, that he would suffocate if he tried to climb out of his dream, out of the sea into the air. Commit yourself to the destructive element and by the exertion of your arms and legs keep yourself up. To that effect. Words like that.'

The Chinese Love Pavilion, I, I

The dream that Brent has been flung into is the dream of India, transmitted to him through his father by his grandfather's watercolours of the Punjab. Saxby intuits this fact from a study of the

water-colours, then from a personal history he extracts from
Brent. It becomes clear that Saxby's wisdom springs from bitter
disillusionment. He isolates Brent's romantic temperament, his
falling in love with the unseen, and encourages him to immerse
himself in his dream of India: 'It's only in dreams you get
anywhere near the truth.' The truth he identifies with 'God, a
heaven, an emotional continuum after death' which we should
spend our natural lives pursuing. The aim is to establish a
'condition of readiness . . . to see all that was allowed to be seen,
prove all that it was permitted to prove here on earth of what
existed beyond it'. It is necessary for the romantic to pursue this
aim because only by doing so will he come near to discovering his
soul, *recognising* himself as the person he otherwise only *felt* himself
to be in life.

Much of Saxby's conversation sounds pretentious and opaque.
It verges on the insane when he begins to talk about the bits of
soul in the table they are talking across, chipped off from the soul
of the tree from which it was made. After Brent's last meeting
with him he does go mad, possibly in his private vendetta against
the Japanese and their Malayan collaborators; certainly, if the
account offered of him at second hand is true, when he becomes
the flower dreamer of the jungle, dreaming his souls into five
flowers and hunting down his enemies who have destroyed the
flowers, or allowed them to fade. But the important point about
Saxby is that although he had never had a dream of his own to fall
into (as Brent says) he is adept at intuiting the dreams of others,
and at thwarting their conscious intentions to resist them. They
are encouraged to commit themselves to the destructive element.
And, as usual in Scott's work, the dream is not merely an illusion.
Or, if it is, it is an illusion reality cannot do without. After all,
Saxby has defined it as a full recognition of what we feel ourselves
to be – failing the fullest recognition of all, which comes only after
death, when 'we would recognise ourselves as the people we felt
ourselves to be in life'. It is not altogether an idiosyncratic
aspiration. It is felt, for example, by Major Reid, Brent's
company commander at Bukit Kallang, when he ruminates
about his 'boys' to Brent after they first hear about Saxby and the
flowers. Reid wonders where his company will be a year from
now, and where he will be. 'When you're not sure what it is
you've got, what it is you've *made*, how do you hold on to it?'

Brent answers, 'Perhaps you shouldn't try.' But Reid can't accept this. 'Ah then', he said, 'you're nothing. Nothing.' In Reid, too, the romantic impulse to complete self-discovery is urgent and uncompromising.

The tragedy of Saxby is that he has never believed in the romantic dream for himself, and he has been losing his grip on its reality for other people during the time after Brent left him in Bombay. When Brent visits him in Singapore, after spending four unproductive years at Graystone's valley, Saxby has lapsed into a world of illusions. He claims he has got used to the idea that he doesn't exist except in the physical sense, and that the illusion of the soul (which is the illusion of palpable identity and human reality) has been brought about merely by 'what we might call the misunderstood mechanical or chemical processes of our bodies'. It seems, therefore, richly and poetically appropriate that after his degeneration into 'the Shaman of the Red Beard', searching for his souls only in the shapes of plants, he should at last be discovered, dead, in a bungalow that has become strangled with overgrown vegetation and transformed into a shrine of flowers:

> Entering it I smelt the death smell that is like the smell lime trees make when their pale, creamy flowers turn brittle and yellow. It was dark, for here the plants choked the windows, clawed at the walls and ceiling as though to break through them and burgeon upwards, higher and higher to face heaven proudly. I cried aloud when I saw him resting on his bed of flowers and hid my face, sickened by his smell and the look he had of being shaped from earth. *The Chinese Love Pavilion*, iii, 6

The story of Saxby and the story of Teena Chang intersect when Saxby tries to use Teena and the love pavilion to identify collaborators and contrive the murder of Japanese soldiers. Teena's unwillingness to comply with his demands (at the time of her affair with Hakinawa) has made her the object of his insane revenge. Brent, deeply in love with Teena, is determined to hunt down Saxby before he can carry out his threat. Though the plot neatly dovetails the fortunes of Brent, Saxby, Teena and Reid, I find it difficult to understand what the invasion of the pavilion by Saxby means in terms of Scott's evidently symbolic intention.

This is probably because of the inadequacies of the writing about
the pavilion, once it becomes absorbed into the narrative and
made the location of Brent's and Teena's less-than-fully-
convincing love affair. A passage in the Prologue beckons
towards a solution. Teena prepares to offer her services to Brent
in either her 'European' or her 'Chinese' mood:

> But once in my arms the mood, whichever it had been, seemed
> to melt away and leave behind it a joy, a sadness, the nature of
> which you never quite understood. I used to think of it as the
> third and final artifice, the professional mystery, the creation
> for you of Teena as a woman waiting for, capable of, love,
> ready to find it in you if you would find it in her.
>
> 'Prologue'

The betrayal of Teena by Brent at the end of the novel recalls to
us the mystery of her lovemaking, which was also a kind of
reality-making, in the course of which she had used, and then
discarded, the artifices of the pavilion. At all events in the
pavilion, with its exotic, and perhaps vulgar, ritual, the two
modes of femininity become one; and then, with the appropriate
lover, blend into a self-defining love for Teena and for Brent.
Presumably the same was true in the past for Hakinawa.

Saxby's flight from dreamless nihilism into murder and
madness must discover, in symbolic terms, its greatest resistance
in the pavilion. By accident, Brent prevents Saxby from carrying
out his plan of destruction. But the destruction comes about
afterwards, in ambiguous circumstances, when Teena is killed
after making love with Reid's new *protégé*, a young soldier called
Sutton. She might have killed herself after Brent betrayed her (by
not taking her away from Bukit Kallang). Or Sutton might have
killed her because 'he had not proved himself a man' and didn't
want his callowness and inexperience to be discovered. Either
way the threat of Saxby's unbelief had, in more prosaic terms
than he had intended, removed her from her own dream – and
presumably destroyed Brent's dream too. It was by the *kris* Brent
had given her at the most satisfactory period of their lovemaking
that she died. But, behind Sutton's hand, Saxby's was the hand
that administered the blow. Brent finishes his story by confessing:
'Sometimes I think that Saxby, in the end, did not fail in the

business of killing her.' Brent's relationship with her was fatally compromised by his quest for Saxby who, whilst having given him much in the past, was now in a position only to take away.

THE BIRDS OF PARADISE (1962)

Scott's failure in *The Chinese Love Pavilion* lay in giving too little substance to the actual relationship between Brent and Teena Chang. The symbolic ambiance of his pavilion remained intact but the human transactions that went on inside it lacked subtlety, and the time and space to be satisfactorily developed. The dialogue inside the tantalisingly mysterious décor failed to convince. What was destroyed with Teena's death never came into focus. We were left with a location and a history capable of evoking the shades of an ambiguous Paradise under threat, but without the density of human contact that would have made it fictionally serviceable.

This is what Scott triumphantly avoided in his next novel, *The Birds of Paradise* – almost certainly his finest pre-*Raj* achievement. Here the narrative is simple, the pattern of prospect and retrospect unforced and necessary, and the central image of the birds of paradise is tightly woven into the structure of the narrative and beautifully appropriate to the states of mind the novel explores. The exposition of a series of related themes through the slow unfolding of several narratives seems to be the ideal medium of Scott's mature art. If Paradise is to be the subject of a writer's fiction, that fiction cannot exist in a present tense alone. It requires the play of memory, the act of the mind looking back into the past and separating deception from truth, teasing out the different forms of truth from the illusions that may have housed them. This recognition of how the truth of the past fades and reshapes itself in the interests of the present is at the heart of Scott's novel. Also at the heart of it is the fact that what a man might suppose is the essential nature of his present may be as illusory as the idealised past it has been built on; and that to see the past differently, from the perspective of a new experience, might be a powerful means of redirecting and reshaping his present. A man can live too much and too little in the past. Certainly he can become too absorbed in paradisaical illusions out of which, in some cases, his past has been fabricated.

We first meet William Conway, the hero of *The Birds of Paradise*, on Manoba, a volcanic island situated off the coast of New Guinea. It soon becomes obvious to us that there are two Manobas: the Manoba of the coastline and trading station, with the SIAT (Straits Islands and Archipelago Trading Company) plantations in the background and hutments and makeshift docks on the edge of the water; and the Manoba of the interior, which is a land of rumour and mystery, 'a dark forgotten island whose warriors challenge your approach, make magic out of tins and mysteries out of birds'. Conway lives near the plantation, having taken a year's sabbatical leave from his job in London in order to visit friends and acquaintances in India and the Far East whom he knew as a child or, later, as a POW in a Japanese camp. One of his fellow prisoners, Cranston, has settled another ex-POW, Daintree, on the island; and certain of the details of Daintree's history have brought Conway there to meet him. Together they set off on expeditions to view the birds of paradise, which are supposed to inhabit the centre of the island. But it may be that they are among the birds out of which the natives have made mysteries. By the end of the novel Conway has never found them. The nearest he comes to them is to hear their song, probably imitated by the village boys, 'for my benefit'. Though neither the natives nor the two other white men on the island will admit that the birds are gone, it is almost certain that the mysteries of the interior in which the *paradisaeidae* play such a significant part are entirely illusory.

The story begins with an anecdote about a parrot called Melba, a bird which is very definitely alive and, in its way, impressive:

> If Melba interrupts her South American love song, and squawks, 'Wurrah Yadoor – a!' I take no notice . . . but if the squawk is followed by the tinny sound she makes with her beak and claws when she tangles with the wire-netting of her cage I leave the hut and go into the clearing to calm her down by tickling her stomach and ruffling the top of her head.
>
> *The Birds of Paradise*, I, I

So far as the story is concerned, Melba is both a consolation and an embarrassment to Conway. She has been given to him as a present by two childhood friends, Dora Salford and Krishanramarao, after his return to Jundapur – one of the Indian Princely States he knew well in his boyhood. The parrot had got used to imitating his name, and 'Krishi' had said that he couldn't bear the thought of her going through life shouting 'William Conway' unless she had William Conway close at hand to hear. 'Love's path never ran smoothly, he said, but there were limits to the obstacles that should be put in its way.' So Melba becomes Conway's personal gift, in a way his lover. He says that 'the parrot would be my personal bird of paradise' and later (to Cranston) that she is a 'mock bird of paradise, the only bird that could easily be obtained living, unless you visited islands like Manoba'. Clearly Melba's presence is of considerable emblematic significance. By looking into the circumstances of Conway's reception of her, and therefore of her connection with other, more authentic birds of paradise, we might be able to clarify Scott's attitudes to romance, illusion, and the quest for reality, which lie at the heart of the novel.

Conway had first known Krishi and Dora in Jundapur back in the 1920s and '30s, when he was the son of the British Resident at the palace of the Maharajah of Tradura, and Dora was the daughter of a major stationed in a town just outside the agency territories. Krishanramarao, or 'Krishi', was the eldest son of the Maharajah of Jundapur. William had known Dora in Tradura, and had conducted a juvenile love-affair with her in the grounds of the palace there. They had met Krishi at Kinwar in the winter of 1928–29, shortly before William's departure for England – from which, it transpired, he was never to return till now. The short period of the Kinwar tiger hunt, and William's stay at the palace at Jundapur with Krishi and Dora during the spring of 1929, comprises the thematic centre of the novel. Out of this experience Conway forged the terms of his entry into the adult world. He imprinted on his spirit a picture of what the world was like, or might be like, or might, in the future, seem to have been like, which was to shake down into the basic elements of his adult personality.

One of the most important strands in this experience is William's feeling for Dora. We know that his marriage with Anne is going to end in bitterness and, eventually, separation. But the initial attraction between the two of them is never described. All the romance and adoration William ever feels for a woman has to do with Dora. It is present in the description of their chaste kiss under the cedar tree (or was it by the gate in the red brick wall?) during the Rajah's garden party. Much more so, it accounts for William's inability to shoot the tiger when it surprises him with Dora in a *machan* up in the Kinwar hills. As the tiger emerges from the shadow and stares, curiously aroused, so William is moved to stare at Dora's profile. The 'waves of enchantment' which spread from this double experience of attention drain away his lust for the animal's blood, and leave him with a lucid realisation of the existence of the girl, and the tiger, and himself. Only on one occasion, much later in the narrative, and as a part of a quite separate passage of reminiscence, does William admit that in a way he loved Dora. But the silent vigil in the *machan* carries a conviction about his feeling for her, and her reality as a person in his eyes, that requires no banal, because overt, acknowledgement. Romantically, it is authenticated a little later by a strange and stirring event. Exercising his horse on the *maidan*, William sees in the distance a dim host of riders wheeling round and round a speck of white that is gradually identified as Dora. Immediately he speeds into the wind towards them, towards the forbidden territory at the other side of the *maidan*, like a lancer 'arm extended forward and out, the hand holding the crop like a sword'. Of course it never happened: not as a real event, not even as a varnished, half-forgotten memory. Both of these would now be no more than pictures in the mind. But between the two extremes represented by such pictures, says Conway, lie others: 'mysterious, magical, tenacious and insubstantial as dreams'. The event on the *maidan* was such a dream, evoking the essence of Conway's youthful passion for Dora at Kinwar.

  The full impact of Jundapur cannot be separated from Krishi's involvement in the relationship between William and Dora. William's feeling for Krishi is compounded of the most complex and self-contradictory impulses: his protection of his father's honour; his jealousy of Krishi's association with Dora; his sense of racial superiority (but uncertain social status in the palace); and his sentimental affection for the Princely States which Krishi, in a way, represents. Between them, Dora and Krishi embody a reality and an illusion of India. Their residence together at the palace infuses a new and powerful life into feelings for India, hitherto of duty and imperial responsibility, that have already been so assiduously cultivated in him by his father and his tutor. When the possibility of a future in India is taken away from him much later, in his uncle's home back in England, it is no wonder that William's sense of loss is so devastating. Not only is his sense of purpose and vocation thwarted. The living centre of his imaginative life has been destroyed at a blow.

William's experience at Jundapur brings about a deepening and a poetic colouring of his attachment to India that has already been awakened by his father and by his knowledge of the history of his family's service in the sub-continent. That history has to do with what seem to be ineradicable family characteristics, passed down from father to son. There are several scenes in the second and third 'Books' of *The Birds of Paradise* (i.e. those parts of the novel which are set neither on Manoba nor in Tradura and Jundapur) which stress the fact of determination. On one occasion Scott calls it 'the tyranny of the genes':

> I think of them as working their silent, counter-revolutionary way into the rebel stronghold of our privacy, imposing and reimposing on us thought and behaviour that ought to be dead and done with. That look of my own father which I sometimes saw in Stephen is a look I feel I have left to grow stronger in him now that I have deserted him. *The Birds of Paradise*, II, I

But what lies behind the 'look'? The way one's inheritance is determined is obscured by two facts. The first is uncertainty about what precisely *is* the moral quality that the 'look' represents (or does it misrepresent it? Is it a pose, a protection against facts of personality which need to be hidden away and forgotten?). This is a question William constantly asks himself about his strangely retiring, withdrawn, and reserved father. Again it is a question he puts to himself in the biological terms of a genetic inheritance:

> When I look from him [his grandfather] to this son, my father, my father stares back at me with two faces: first with the face of the boy who wanted for himself exactly what his father wanted for him and moved passionately and icily towards it, then with

the face of a boy who wanted something else, a boy to whom an
Indian career was a living death, a cold and bitter duty he
would support only because the genes had made him prone to
the call of duty and had shaped him to endure cold. Either face
could be the real face, and although the evidence weighs
heavily against the second there are times when it puts in a
stronger appeal.   *The Birds of Paradise*, II, 2

Even if the evidence does weigh heavily against the second face,
William's inheritance is still complicated by the other fact he
needs to take account of: that the inheritance is not a single, but a
double one. To see both himself and his son as they 'really' are he
must not overlook what might have been passed on to them from
Robert Conway's wife, who died when William was six, and,
more significantly perhaps, from his own paternal grandmother.
This woman, called 'Little Ma' by the rest of the family, was very
different, in both physical build and temperament, from her
elder son (William's father) and her daughter Sarah. Her short
stature and fatness have been passed on to William's Uncle
Walter, the younger son, who was born in England and who
remained there as a prosperous businessman, with the exception
of the years he spent in Northern France during the Great War.
So when William is brooding on his family inheritance, although
he longs to find in himself what he believes he sees in his father – a
devotion to duty, a spareness, an ability to comprehend the world
in a clear, hard light – there is always his father's second face, and
his grandmother's face behind it, that obscures the single vision of
himself that it is his ambition to hold and preserve.

    Uncle Walter is a living reminder of the 'flaw' in his
inheritance. Living at his house, 'Four Birches', as he does from
the age of eleven onwards (after his return from India), William
has ample opportunity to assess the other aspect of the family
inheritance which is so firmly lodged in his uncle. More than
that, when William's Indian ambitions are destroyed and he
enters into a more adult relationship with Walter, he sees that
Walter, with all his comfortable middle-class unsusceptibility to
the strange and the exotic, might have understood something of
the rest of the family's involvement with India that they had
never learned at all, or that they had learned only at the very end
of their lives. At this stage William sees Walter as 'a man who

might have intentionally cut himself adrift from the firmly anchored tradition of service in the glittering heart of an Empire because he saw it not as an anchored tradition but as the hung-on-to balloon I was trying not to yell for'. He recognises the good that has been done by people like his brother, William's father, but has decided that, in India, the bad has far outweighed it. For Robert Conway, as his brother sees it, India has been 'part and parcel of the illusion of him but now the illusion was breaking up, losing all its protective skins as my eyes bored into them and peeled them away to get at the reality . . .'.

In his schooldays Robert Conway had been given the nickname 'Old Very Light', after the flares produced by a Very pistol during the war. These enabled the soldiers to tell what was alive (i.e. moving) and what was lifeless (i.e. inert), in what would otherwise have been a pitch-black landscape. Presumably Conway had the effect of a Very light on the people around him, and the effect persisted into adult life in the Colonial service. 'However turbulent a condition a state or group of states was in, it became calm almost directly he arrived, as if people froze in their tracks at his approach.' The snag in this otherwise highly desirable attribute lay in the illusory nature of the world in which it forced the man who possessed it to live. In the war, soldiers were ordered to freeze when a Very flare was sent up from the opposite camp, to appear immobile like a tree or a bush or a boulder – since the impression of movement was the only sign of life the enemy would be looking for in the brief period of the flare. So Conway's Very light – permanently switched on, as it were – created precisely that illusory world his son has been trying to take away from his own son (stripping his bedroom of dolls and toys) in order to make him more like his grandfather. Later he is able at least partially to accept that this is what he has done. He admits that: 'It was the illusion of Father that I loved, the concept of the embodiment of what I was to be.' But his father has prevented him from being that. He has not allowed him to return to India and has put him to work with his Uncle Walter instead. For this reason William begins to see his father differently. As he grows older, he says, 'I felt my father grow smaller, saw him in my mind's eye shrink into the actual mould of being a human being, the bottle from which as a child I had caused him to rise like a genie.'

It is not surprising that later in his life Conway should continue
to nurture an ambition to test the illusion which the inheritance
he had received from his father had built around him; and that
his experience with Dora and Krishi at Jundapur had seemed to
invest with a poetic, even mythical substance. At first he applies
the test to Cranston, the Quaker doctor he knew in the prison
camp at Pig Eye; and to Daintree, Cranston's friend and mentor,
now working for SIAT on Manoba. But in each of these cases the
work that was their life is no longer available or no longer
satisfies. 'The illusion of my life had been that a man should love
his job, be dedicated to it, born to it.' This was what he thought
he had found, in reality, in Cranston's medical work at Pig Eye;
and what Cranston thought he had found in Daintree's struggle
to eradicate yaws from the Malayan jungle tribes. But it was an
illusion nevertheless. After 1945, Cranston's work was over.
When penicillin was discovered, Daintree's struggle became
futile. So Conway has to move further into the past, into his own
past, into the heart of the illusion where, strangely, it may be that
what is most real to him, his own reality, might be found. 'I
hadn't killed the past by going back to Jundapur. I hadn't buried
my dead. The dead weren't dead. Everything had grown directly
out of the past, undeviatingly; you could squint from the rather
blowsy flower down the stem and see the living root; a root which
had shaped me . . .' And this takes him back again to the palace
at Jundapur, to Dora and Krishi, and to the birds of paradise.

The birds perched on branches of trees and shrubs in a
spacious hexagonal cage constructed in the middle of an island
on the Rajah of Jundapur's estate. Though the roof was hollow,
looking up at it Krishi, Dora and William could see the
paradisaeidae suspended there, or swooping, hovering and soaring
above the leaves and branches of their natural forest. Beneath
them, in a glass-topped cabinet, was a set of coloured drawings of
the birds, with an account of their habits and the curious legends
that surround them.

But the birds were dead, stuffed; brought to the island stuffed
and dead years before by the Rajah's father.

Periodically a Muslim servant called Akbar Ali, using a tall
step ladder which could be unclasped from the walls of the
cage, climbed up and unscrewed the birds from their rods one

by one, and brought them down to inspect the wire frames. In
the leather bag he brought there were coils of wire, pliers, a pot
of Vaseline jelly and little bottles of fluid which he applied to
the body feathers . . .   *The Birds of Paradise*, I, 7

Like the primitive make-up Krishi and William painted themselves with to enact the story of Krishna and the Indian princess's
brother, the jellies and lotions that Ali applied to the birds,
imparting to them their magnificent gloss and splendour, betrays
a hint of tawdriness, of artifice at the heart of experience. It is a
more successful bringing together of the significant and the
absurd, the urgent and the theatrically cosmetic, than was
represented by the Chinese pavilion in the earlier novel. More
successful because the subtle blend of nostalgia, romance, and
inner, emotional reality the birds represent is so satisfyingly
reproduced in the behaviour of the three characters to one
another both then, in the past, and now, during Conway's period
of return – when Dora is still, surprisingly, a guest at Jundapur,
and the birds of paradise remain undisturbed in their gorgeous
but stilted postures.

William and Dora row to the island one afternoon and re-enter
the cage. Though Ali has been dead for two years, from the
ground there is no sign of decay. By now there has been an
explicit identification of the birds as symbols of the raj, and of the
Princely States during the British occupation of India. But it has
become clear that they mean very much more than that, on a
personal level, to William and Dora – though what they mean is
intimately tied up with William's and Dora's Indian history and
background. What they most profoundly represent is brought
out by a picture of one of the birds, an engraving in the old
cabinet entitled 'Natives of Aru shooting the Great Bird of
Paradise'. Here the first victim lies on the ground stunned by the
blunt tip of an arrow, waiting to be killed in a way that won't
damage its plumage or reduce the market value of its skin.
Looking at the engraving, Conway's mind slips back thirty years,
to the moment when he first saw it. Those thirty years are 'sucked
back into the vacuum their going had created', and he is back by
the side of Dora, watching her profile in the way he watched it in
the *machan* during the tiger hunt. All the illusions of imperial
splendour, the dreams of a past in India that might have been –

even in a simulated form in the Princely States with their ossified and irrelevant splendours – drain away from the memory and the fantasy of those thirty years. But they have helped to bring back the truth of William's feeling for Dora, disentangled from the fantasy that will always be incomplete, because involved with so much that was real and lasting: 'The . . . lines at the corners of her eyes . . . , the husky memsahib voice became, briefly, focuses for my tenderness, and acquired beauty as did all the traces left on her by her years, for her years were her life, and I had loved her as a child.'

The myths and legends of the birds go much further to complicate our feeling for what Conway has lost and the illumination he has now, fleetingly, achieved. No one can say how seriously their mythical powers were taken by the natives who hunted them and sold them, or how far they cultivated their air of mystery as a merely commercial asset. The belief that they were footless ('Apoda') emphasised their ethereal, immaterial potentialities. Or the suspicion that their feet were cut off by native traders merely emphasised the brutal retribution men exact from whatever is beautiful and strange. The power of the birds, even when their dead forms are capable of giving wing only to fantasy and dreams in the hearts of mortal men, is demonstrated in the strangely isolated moments William, Dora and Krishi remember having experienced in the cage. One of them was always absent, and in the minds of the two who were present there was always a difference of opinion about what had happened between them.

Conway's return to Jundapur and his journey to Manoba are stages in a search for what might lie behind the *maya* he suspects his father thought was all, finally, life had to offer. At first he looks for the importance a man might possess in his own eyes; then in the histories of others – in Cranston, and, on Manoba, in Daintree. But the most substantial object of his quest remains, in a sense, the most fanciful – the birds of paradise which, if they existed and were found, would make the illusory splendours of his past take wing. If they do not exist, and are only the fabrications of Daintree's good humour and the vocal tricks of native boys, there is still Melba, the mock bird of paradise, singing of the hills, valleys and forests of her youth. She 'sings as though she sees them through her wrinkled, lidded eyes, which she half closes. There is

contentment in her singing, happiness in recollection and a
mature acceptance that so much of her youth was *maya*, so much
of it illusion.'

She was given to Conway by Dora and Krishi, a token of
something that persists out of the past, out of thirty years ago.
And she squawks, from them, his name: 'William Conway! and
Wurrah Yadoor-a!' 'I feel that it is my youth she has been singing
and not her own and at times like this I go up to her cage and we
stare at each other and try to break down the terrible barrier that
exists between man and beast.'

THE CORRIDA AT SAN FELÍU (1964)

This is Scott's most puzzling book. Most of it is written in the form
of a novel, *The Plaza de Toros*, which is about the marital and
professional problems of an ageing novelist called Edward
Thornhill. This is a first-person, almost entirely autobiographical
narrative, recalling Thornhill's past in India and England, and
exploring the connections between that past and the circumstances of his present life in Spain, where he is living with his wife,
Myra, at a villa in Playa de Faro, a holiday resort on the Costa
Brava.

The autobiographical narrative is interspersed with fragments
of another novel Thornhill is trying to write. In it, the details of
his life with Myra and, earlier, with his cousin John, are
transformed into a story about two characters he calls Bruce and
Thelma Craddock. But his ability to write this story about the
Craddocks is compromised by two events, widely separated in
time, but closely related in Thornhill's mind by an oppressive
sense of guilt and shame. The event in the past over which he feels
a strong sense of guilt is his 'theft' of Myra from his cousin John, to
whom she was engaged, and who died in a car crash shortly after
her elopement with Thornhill. The event in the present which
instils in him a tormenting combination of jealousy, shame, and a
feeling of deserved retribution, is his discovery that a clandestine
sexual relationship is being conducted between Myra and a
young Spanish boy.

The Plaza de Toros informs us that Thornhill's novel is never
completed. After an unpleasant scene with Myra, in which he

accuses her of infidelity with the 'godling', Thornhill attends a corrida in the nearby town of San Felíu. After this the novel ends, in so far as it is concerned directly with Edward Thornhill's problems. An additional three pages contain fragments of a fresh attempt at his novel about the Craddocks.

But Thornhill's novel begins only a third of the way through *The Corrida at San Felíu*. It is preceded by four passages of narrative and a personal memoir about Thornhill, who, it appears, died in a car crash shortly after completing *The Plaza de Toros*. So the autobiographical novel Thornhill says he failed to complete in the narrative of *The Plaza de Toros*, he actually did complete as *The Plaza de Toros* itself. Therefore, not only is *The Plaza de Toros* made available to the reader, but so are the four related passages of narrative that were discovered among his literary remains. These take the form of two complete short stories and two alternative openings of a novel about Bruce and Thelma Craddock (two people 'turning up in disgrace'), one of which bears some slight resemblance (via connections between the characters) to the second of the short stories. Naturally, all four pieces of narrative bear heavily on the autobiographical narrative that Thornhill offers us in his novel, *The Plaza de Toros*.

I confess I cannot think of a less welcoming advertisement for a work of fiction than the summary provided above. It makes the *Corrida* sound like the worst kind of experimental novel: sterile, over-elaborate, a novel about a novelist writing a novel within a novel, derivative – Hemingway and all those bulls. But a careful reading of the full text – fragments, stories, novel and final fragment – will almost certainly correct any such impression. The whole novel, not just the *Plaza*, is a disturbingly original treatment of some of Scott's familiar themes: the loss of Paradise, now glimpsed as an idea in the mind, of which any lived reality must fall intolerably short; the deceptions men and women play on each other in what must be far from ideal sexual re-lationships; the distortion of reality in the interests of both responsible and irresponsible functions of the imagination; and the ways in which men strive to exert power over one another.

The short stories, 'The Leopard Mountain' and 'The First Betrayal', are both very good stories in their own right. The fragments that follow are not so good and genuinely do appear to be passages from work in progress which is failing to find a proper direction. But the real value of both the stories and the fragments lies in their relationship with Edward Thornhill's past life, as it is summarised in the Preface and, more importantly, as it is fully developed in the semi-fiction of the *Plaza*. The reason why the novel could not have appeared in any form but the one in which it does appear is that its main subject is the attempt by Thornhill to be true to his past, and, by being true to his past, honestly to confront his present. It is the story of a man's effort to know himself in circumstances which provide any number of distractions from that effort – distractions in the form of fictional transformations which obscure important truths, or which omit, distort, mistime, dislocate events which need to be viewed in a special order for their real significance to be disclosed. Hence Thornhill's jealousy when he discovers the presence of the godling with his wife on the beach below their villa affects his awareness not merely of his present circumstances but of his past as well, when he himself had adopted the godling's role in relation to Myra and John.

Facts like these have their effect on the way Thornhill writes about the relationship between Bruce and Thelma Craddock. They also are guilty of sexual infidelities, the nature of which subtly change as Thornhill's growing awareness of Thelma's betrayal persuades him to rearrange the patterns of his fiction. For example, most of the time Bruce and Thelma are evidently substitutes for himself and Myra. But at other times, when Thornhill's sense of impotence and humiliation over Myra and the godling is very sharply felt, the novelist sees himself in the role of one of the other characters: Bruce's cousin Nigel for example, whose engagement to Thelma is destroyed by Bruce's greater sexual attractiveness. On another occasion Thornhill's memory of the failure of his first marriage (with a Jewish girl called Mitzi whom he got out of Nazi Germany before the holocaust, but who killed herself six months later) impinges on his present emotional frustration. One of the results of this is that he composes a vivid account of Bruce Craddock's first marriage with a Eurasian girl, Leela, who kills herself, like Mitzi, six months after their marriage.

Significantly it is Nigel who tells the story of Leela's death at Mahwar, thus providing one explanation of the Craddocks' appearance in disgrace in one of the introductory fragments. It is

significant also that in the first version of the Craddocks'
appearance in disgrace, they turned up not in Mahwar but in the
Playa, and behaved as if they were not disgraced at all. This was
because Thornhill's sense of guilt over what he did to John when
he robbed him of Myra has been exacerbated by the way the
whole thing is now happening to him, at the hands of the godling.
So the Bruce Craddock who accompanies Thelma to the Playa
del Mar is not Edward at all, but John – the younger man whose
twenty-year advantage over Edward would presumably have
made the godling unnecessary and expendable.

It would be tedious to rehearse all the details of the subtle
interplay between fact and fiction in this novel. Sufficient to say
that it gives the narrative an impetus that develops credibly out of
Thornhill's obsessive concern with his personal problems. In the
end the interaction of his private circumstances with his handling
of the story of the Craddocks drives him, almost it seems
inevitably, to the corrida he had sought for so long to avoid. But
in seeking to avoid the corrida, it is suggested, Thornhill has been
seeking to avoid his destiny. For it is there that he learns what has
been, what is, and what should be the real connection between
his life and his art.

Certainly the corrida must have had a startlingly positive
effect on his ability to write. The Preface has already told us that
the whole of the *Plaza* could have been written only during the
brief interval (little more than a month) between his journey to
San Felíu and his death at Toroella de Sta Barbara. This means
that the new autobiographical cast of the novel was decided upon
immediately after his visit to the corrida. Its form is the direct
consequence of what he discovered there. Its substance, scarcely
separable from the form, is a record of the circumstances that led
to his attendance.

Thornhill's jealousy of Myra and the godling, his suspicions
and fantasies about their relationship, and the effect these
suspicions and fantasies have on the reorganisation of the
material we have already encountered in the fragments and the
short stories – all these features of the *Plaza de Toros* make it clear
that the chaotic uncertainties of life are not to be subsumed in the
formal discipline of a serene and classic art. Nevertheless art, as
distinct from the struggle to create art, might incorporate a kind
of serenity, an order, a paradisaical stasis that no life can ever

contrive for itself. In the bullfight Thornhill discovers symbolic equivalents of many of the features of his own life: the *quaerencia* – the place marked out by the bull as its own territory, not to be entered by a rival with impunity; the *faena* – the final execution of the bull at a place and a time which confer a dignity on its dying. But more important than this, the ritual of the bullfight as a whole can be interpreted as an allegory of human life, on which has been conferred a form and purposeful sequence that life as it is lived does not disclose. In the bullfight Thornhill sees what he calls 'dramatic representations of my own endless struggle to transmute the raw perpetual motion of life into the perfect immobility of art'. But at the same time as he sees this, he sees also that the way the struggle is conducted in the bullring undercuts that final claim. The perfection and immobility are illusory and are seen to be so. For by witnessing the killing of the bull and translating it by death into a symbol of tranquillity (both matador and bull are understood to be *tranquilo* at the end of the *faena*) a man is only snatching at 'an illusory moment of peace':

> But peace itself is an illusion, if by peace we mean something more durable than temporary respite from the prick of ambition, and the soaring and sinking fever of passion. Perhaps it is only in art that this more durable peace is to be found; not in the creation of it – no, not there – but in contemplation of what has been created, endless Edens, shapely worlds, formed out of the terrible void and the deep blue darkness of endless frightening space . . .
>
> *The Corrida at San Felíu*, ii, 9

The corrida is a unique art because it 'defies the law of life arrested by artifice'. The materials out of which the art is composed are real, and each bullfight, though a fresh representation of the tragic quest for peace, is a masterful *exposé* of the insufficiency, the illusory quality, of the object of any such quest. The art of the bullfight is not finally separable from the raw material of life from which all other arts seek to release themselves. Consequently here, as nowhere else, the tragic peace and the strenuous simulation of it in the creation of the tragedy exist simultaneously. This is the art Thornhill seeks to reproduce in his own fiction, with its autobiographical subject and its rapid composition in the middle of the personal chaos it describes. In it, the alternative versions he had experimented with in the first Part are extended, changed and absorbed into the record of the author's present, undisguised preoccupations.

There are, though, at least two moments when, writing about the Craddocks and not himself, Thornhill achieves something of that 'perfect immobility of art' he has been struggling all his life to create. This happens at first in his description of Ampurias, where he has seen Thelma and Bruce, representing Myra and John, imaginatively projected 'into a future that was never theirs'. As they take possession of the terrace on which Thornhill is sitting, the whole scene opens out into a superb re-creation of some classical Eden where all is innocence. What happened between Thornhill and Myra long ago is erased from memory and replaced by what now, he feels, should always have been:

I ate at the Hotel Playa de Faro, out on its pine log and bamboo terrace at a table from which I could see the lights of the Villa Vora la Mar. 'Is that it?' Thelma said. 'But then it must be. It's how I imagined it, how I hoped it would be.' And stood there with Bruce smiling a smile that nothing could destroy, because this Thelma, this Bruce, were romantic figments, at most impossible projections of John and Myra into a future that was never theirs. Piece by piece their harlequin luggage was taken up the hill. Case by case they took possession. If you looked long enough you could just make them out, arm in arm, silhouetted against the light in one of the upstairs rooms, looking down at the little bay that had been scooped out of the shoreline by a white horse from Poseidon's stables, just as two dark-eyed children had looked down in wonder, from just about that spot, at the shape of the hoof and the distant apparition, far out on the horizon, its wet mane gleaming in the sun; centuries ago; long before the advent of a civilization that brought strange gods from across the sea, and altars for the sacrificial killing of bulls, and left their stone relics in Ampurias.

And long before that there had been no bay. The blue-green sea scourged an unbroken line of terracotta coloured rock. Immense trees stood on the hills with their thick branches heaving in the wind, jerking the long bell ropes of the lianas that chained them to ground. In the deep indigo shadows of the trees fleshly plants clothed the hill-sides, stirred by the movement of the ropes and the wild currents of air. Sometimes the sun was obscured by boiling clouds from which rain lashed down and forks of lightning struck, lighting the eyes of serpents coiled watchfully under rocks and in the shallows of the sea. And when the storm of creation had died the serpents emerged and wound their way into the dense carpet of leaf and stalk. Strange birds flew above the trees and the plants were stirred now not by the wind but by the movements of animals.

The Corrida at San Felíu, ii, 7

As always the peace does not last. For 'This was the scene of an arrival too. They came over the hill after a long cold journey and sat warming themselves against a rock; and after a while, not speaking, began to throw stones into the sea, remembering Eden.'

The second time Thornhill achieves the tranquillity that has evaded him in both his life and (with the exception described above) his art, is at the very end of the novel, when he has lost contact altogether with his own story and has resumed the story of the Craddocks turning up in shame at Mahwar. On this occasion, however, the centre of the narrative is not occupied by Bruce Craddock, Thornhill's *alter ego*, but by his wife Thelma and her lover, Ned Pearson – whom Thornhill has until then thrust inconspicuously into the background. Now he opens the narrative to him and directly confronts his possession of Thelma, which is the same thing as John's aborted, and the godling's actual, possession of Myra. Furthermore he does this through Thelma's own consciousness of her relationship with Ned, in all its physical and imaginative detail. The artistic expression Thornhill achieves by this device is at once exhilarating, impersonal, and profoundly unselfish. His description of Thelma's and Ned's lovemaking could have been written only by a man who has escaped from the cage of jealousy and egotism that have hitherto been the most characteristic features of his self-portrait.

... here a union, an awful wholeness has been achieved between man and nature; and so we lie for ever in carved cohabitation, in the dark and in the light, in the rains, through

all the seasons of the year, immortally joined and lying as still
as if we were dead so that the birds light on my nipples and on
my toes, on his neck, his heels and his marble buttocks. They
fly away from us flapping their wings, cooling us in the heat
when we have no moisture to sweat. Centuries pass. My cheeks
and hands and the long curved column of his back are lichened
over. Thunder bounces away from us. The flash of lightning
reveals his face, petrified in its expression of ecstasy. The dew
settles and we lick these tears of heaven with our parched stone
tongues. The heat of the summer scorches our stone bones and
the frosts of winter fracture our stone flesh. But we are joined as
no man and woman were ever joined before, and only the
crack of doom can destroy us. *The Corrida at San Felíu*, ii, 10

The fact that the novel ends on this note might explain why
Thornhill killed himself so soon after completing it. One could
argue that he had accepted the only alternative to a return to the
selfishness, duplicity and suspicion that had gone into the making
of his novel and his life so far. Accordingly he turned from the
tranquillity of art to the only tranquillity that lies outside art –
the permanent tranquillity of death. It is a bitter irony, and a sign
of Scott's ambiguous treatment of Thornhill's character from the
start, that in killing himself he killed Myra too. We alone, as
readers, will be able to weigh the selfishness of that act against the
experience of selfless impersonality Thornhill had distilled into
his art, and encompassed in the last paragraph of the novel we
have read.

4 *The Raj Quartet*

(We must remember the worst because the worst is the lives we
lead, the best is only history, and between our history and our
lives there is this vast dark plain where the rapt and patient
shepherds drive their invisible flocks in expectation of God's
forgiveness.)

The Day of the Scorpion, ii, i, 2

At the moment of writing, the *Raj Quartet* is no more than four
years old. In spite of the very considerable interest in it that has
been taken by the general reading public, the only commentary
of any length that I have found worth reading is Max Beloff's
review of the fourth volume, which appeared in *Encounter* in May
1976. Beloff's approach is, as one would expect, historical. He
entitles his review 'The End of the Raj: Paul Scott's Novels as
History'. The questions to which he wants to know if Scott's
novels provide satisfactory answers are: 'Has [he] succeeded in
making Britain's retreat and the partition of India that followed
it . . . more directly intelligible than these events might otherwise have been to us? Can he convey both what these events meant
to those affected directly by them and their wider significance?
Has he succeeded – where many Indians would argue that E. M.
Forster failed – in apprehending true Indian feeling about
relations with the British?' The opinion of a respected historian
that these are the kinds of questions we should be asking when we
read a novel like *A Division of the Spoils* (the one with which Beloff
is mainly concerned) will be disputed by many critics and some
readers of fiction. But they seem to me to be very pertinent
questions; questions which, for some of the reasons Beloff
suggests, a novelist might be better equipped to answer than a
historian.

In my commentary on this very long and complex sequence of

novels, I shall begin by examining the way they try to make historical events intelligible. Only after I have done that shall I relate this effort to the more private psychological studies they contain, and the metaphysical and ethical themes I have tried to show have dominated Scott's fiction from the beginning. It might be said that the success of the *Quartet* as 'history' (if it is successful as history: Beloff thinks it is) will be a test of the relevance and correctness of those studies and themes. If the characters of the *Quartet* carry with them something approximating to the states of mind and attitudes to reality demonstrated in characters from the earlier novels; and if these states of mind, etc., appropriately varied and reshaped by the particular exigencies of the situation in India between 1942 and 1947, go some way towards explaining why the events of those years fell out as they did – then we shall have before us some evidence not only of the penetration and delicacy of Scott's insights into human behaviour, but of their universality too. This I shall try to demonstrate by showing the close dependence of the political and historical virtues of the *Quartet* on Scott's by now mature understanding of man's ambition and his fate. I shall also try to show how in the *Quartet* Scott carries further his interest in unconventional arrangements of narrative to convey, in all their subtlety and mystery, the details of that dependence.

Before I can do either of these things, however, I shall have to offer a brief résumé of the plot. Reading a book as long as the *Quartet*, divided into four novels whose events overlap and are modified in the light of new information and the benefits of retrospect, is an enjoyable but not an unstrenuous experience. To be reminded of what actually happens in it might be a useful preliminary to the literary historical enquiry that is to follow.

The events of the *Raj Quartet* extend over a period of five years, from the 'Quit India' motion of the All India Congress Committee in August 1942, to the preparations for partition that followed the British retreat in August 1947. The first volume, *The Jewel in the Crown* (1966), traces some of the causes and consequences of two events that occurred during the disturbances that followed the Congress vote. The first of these was the assault on Miss Edwina Crane, a Supervisor of Protestant schools in the Mayapore district; and the murder of her colleague, Mr Chaudhuri, resident teacher at the school in Dibrapur. The second, more lengthily developed event, was the rape of Miss Daphne Manners – the niece of Lady Manners, widow of an ex-governor of Ranpur – by a gang of Indian youths.

In the first Part we are offered a history of Edwina Crane's career in the Indian Education Service, culminating in the violent attack on her on the road from Dibrapur. In Parts 2, 3, and 6 several characters meditate on her experience and offer opinions about the sort of woman she was. In the course of these meditations we learn that she killed herself by dressing in Indian clothes and immolating herself in something like the traditional manner of *suttee*.

The rest of the novel is devoted to the story of Daphne Manners. After her parents' death she has been brought up by Sir Henry and Lady Manners, and is now staying in Mayapore, at the house of an old friend of her aunt called Lili Chatterjee. During this time she enters into two emotional commitments. One of them, with the District Superintendent of Police, Ronald Merrick, is not at all of her choosing, and she eventually refuses an offer of marriage from him. The other, with a young Indian called Hari Kumar, who has been brought up in England and educated at one of its most prestigious public schools, develops into a serious relationship that transports them both across the racial barrier. After consummating their love in the Bibighar Gardens they are set on by the gang of Indians who beat up Kumar and rape Daphne. Merrick tries to pin the crime on Kumar and five of his associates, but certain technical details and, most damagingly, Daphne's refusal to give evidence that would implicate him, make it impossible to charge him with the offence. Nevertheless he is detained in prison under Defence of the Realm ordinances, being 'suspected' by Merrick of subversive activities against the British during the disturbances.

The Day of the Scorpion (1968) touches on the relationship between Daphne and Hari only in passing. We are reminded that Daphne died in childbirth and that Hari remained in the prison at Kandipat. The baby is christened (Parvati) by Lady Manners, and accompanies her on her travels through Northern India, where Lady Manners becomes a byword for eccentricity and un-English behaviour. The only extensive development of the Bibighar affair is an examination of Kumar by a Captain Rowan (in Part One of the second Book) which produces an exhaustive account of the details of Kumar's arrest, detention and treatment at the hands of Ronald Merrick. This treatment, according to Kumar and a fellow detainee, was brutally sadistic, indicating strong homosexual tendencies in Merrick which are at variance with the public image he presents to the world at all other times.

The main narrative of the second volume, however, has to do with the Laytons, an Anglo-Indian military family who did not appear in *The Jewel in the Crown*. Their long-standing involvement with India is documented with profuse details from their family trees and the social-regimental connections they enjoy. Before their removal from Ranpur to Pankot, in the hills, the youngest daughter, Susan, is to marry a captain in the Indian army called Teddie Bingham. The mother, Mildred, feels the strain of responsibility for the marriage: her husband is a POW in Germany. But the wedding takes place without any major upsets in the Princely State of Mirat, where the Nawab, a pro-British progressive who has allowed himself to be guided towards a liberal and democratic constitution by a White Russian *émigré* called Bronowsky, has offered the Laytons the hospitality of his guest house. The only embarrassment occurs when a stone is thrown into the limousine in which Teddie Bingham and his best man are travelling to the service. This best man is Ronald Merrick, now a captain in Military Intelligence, whom Teddie has had to rope in at the last moment after his original choice has gone down with jaundice. The incident of the stone is followed by a distressing scene on the station platform where Merrick is solicited by an Indian woman in a white saree who pleads with him, falls on her knees, and places her forehead on the ground before his feet. These are the first signs that Merrick's treatment of Kumar and the other boys has not been forgotten. Further details of the hounding of Merrick by young Indian activists, intent on making political capital out of the Kumar case, are given in the second Part of *The Towers of Silence*.

Before the wedding, when the Laytons were spending the summer in Kashmir, the elder Layton sister, Sarah (who now emerges as one of the most important charcters in the *Quartet*), visits Lady Manners secretly on her houseboat at Srinagar, and sees the baby Parvati. After the wedding she discusses the Kumar case with Merrick. Though she dislikes him, she begins to form a relationship with him that is further developed as a result of events that occur shortly after the wedding. After getting Susan pregnant during their honeymoon at Nanoora, Teddie goes off with his regiment on active service, and is killed whilst on re-connaissance. Merrick, who was with him at the time, tried to save him, but was badly burned and mutilated. At Susan's request Sarah visits him in hospital at Calcutta. There she hears the details of Merrick's relationship with Teddie. While staying with her Aunt Fenny in Calcutta, Sarah is seduced by a compulsive womaniser called Clarke. On her way home to Pankot, waiting to change trains at Ranpur station, she is entertained by Count Bronowsky and Captain Rowan in the Nawab's private carriage.

Whilst at Mirat, Sarah has formed a friendly, though distant, relationship with the Count's protégé, Ahmed Kasim, the second son of a prominent Congress (though Muslim) politician now incarcerated by the British in the fort at Premanagar. His arrest, his interview with the British authorities, and his relation to Congress and the members of his family, comprise the first Part of *The Day of the Scorpion*. His history and that of his two sons are taken up again in the last volume of the *Quartet*, where the Muslim dilemma over partition or absorption into the new Independent State of India is dealt with at great length.

Very little new information about the main characters is provided by *The Towers of Silence* (1971). We hear something of Teddie Bingham's dealings with Ronald Merrick in the canton- ment before the wedding. Also we discover that Sarah has been made pregnant by her liaison with Clarke, and has to go to Aunt Fenny's in Calcutta for an abortion. In the meantime Susan gives birth to a baby boy, and falls into a dangerous state of post-natal depression. Finally, Ronald Merrick appears in Pankot to pay his respects to the Layton family. That is all that happens that is new concerning the Laytons and their circle. Kumar, Kasim, Ahmed – none of the Indian characters puts in an appearance. Even Lady Manners, a tenuous presence throughout the *Quartet*, appears only in fleeting glimpses, as a signature in the Governor's visiting book when she enters and leaves Pankot.

The presiding genius of *The Towers of Silence* is Barbie Batchelor, an old acquaintance of Edwina Crane. She has been accepted by Mabel Layton, Sarah and Susan's great aunt, as a paying guest at her home in Pankot. Barbie's loyalty to Mabel, and her evident unselfishness and good nature, serve as an

admirable touchstone against which to measure the behaviour of
the rest of the English community in Pankot. She throws a great
deal of light on the strained relations between Mabel and her
stepdaughter Mildred, and she discloses Mildred's reliance upon
Sarah to keep her from degenerating into alcoholism and sexual
dissipation. Also Barbie's association with Miss Crane, developing into a morbid obsession as her health deteriorates and the
news of her old colleague becomes more and more disturbing,
eventually turns into an intermittent self-identification with the
dead woman. In this way we are provided with yet another
example of the disintegration of character brought about by the
manner in which a personality in many ways distinguished, and
certainly distinctive, is affected by the Indian experience.

The fourth novel, *A Division of the Spoils* (1975), carries the story
forward to the British retreat in 1947. A new character, Guy
Perron, is introduced. He is a sergeant in Field Security, and acts
as a medium through which many of the reflections on the
historical significance of what is happening are communicated.
Perron is also an interesting character in his own right, and he is
brought into contact with Ronald Merrick and Sarah Layton in
ways that tell us a great deal more about both of these familiar
landmarks of the *Quartet*. Also Nigel Rowan's contribution to the
story becomes more important. He is now ADC to the provincial
Governor. As such he becomes involved in the neutralisation of
Mohammed Kasim's political ambitions and in Bronowsky's
efforts to persuade the Nawab of Mirat to have his territories
included in the new independent Indian state. He also has to deal
with the backwash of the Kumar case as it affects Ronald
Merrick and, through him, large numbers of less important
characters who are subject to Merrick's authority. One of these
characters is Mohammed Kasim's younger son Sayed, who has
defected to the Indian National Army and is now in Merrick's
custody. Another is one of Colonel Layton's old havildars,
Muzzafir Khan, who commits suicide as a result of Merrick's
treatment of him (as a defector to the Japanese). Eventually
Merrick, who has married Susan Layton only a year before, is
killed by certain anonymous young men who have attached
themselves to him at Pankot. He is strangled, and then hacked to
pieces with an axe.

A great many other things happen in this long novel. Colonel

Layton returns to Pankot. Sarah Layton forms an attachment with Guy Perron. Perron is involved in several adventures in Bombay and Pankot under the watchful eye of Merrick and his Pathan servant – comically described as the 'Red Shadow'. (Indeed, there is a great deal more comedy in this book than there is in the other members of the *Quartet*.) Bronowsky plans to create a new political order in Mirat by marrying Shiraz, the Nawab's only daughter, to his protégé, Ahmed (who is, after all, a member of the illustrious Kasim family). And there is the final, awful débâcle on the train from Mirat to Ranpur, in which conflict between the races gets out of control and Ahmed is killed by a marauding band of Sikhs and Hindus.

The *Quartet* ends, in human terms, where it began: with a dead Indian on the road, being tended by representatives of the English ruling class who are powerless to help him. In the first instance there was a single victim, the nominally Christian Mr Chaudhuri; in the last, the Muslim victims spread out into the distance on either side of the arrested train. It is an imbalance which gives some indication of the solemnity and often depressive quality of Scott's vision of life. But it also conforms with strict accuracy to the movement of events between August of 1942 and the other August of five years later.

In a novel which contains so many reflections by so many characters on the British experience of India it may seem invidious to select one passage as a summary of Scott's point of view. Indeed it is impossible to do this because his point of view is not a polemical one. It is not a straightforward endorsement of certain actions and principles and a critique of others, from some Olympian eminence of political and moral wisdom. But one has to start somewhere. And it seems to me that one of the most eminently sensible statements of the dilemma in which both English and Indians found themselves during the years leading up to Independence is contained in one of Guy Perron's notebooks. A note he makes after he has come home from the deplorable party with which *A Division of the Spoils* opens, when he finds his flat-mate Leonard Purvis bleeding into his bath after an unsuccessful attempt at suicide, is probably the fullest expression of his point of view. The tawdriness of the Maharanee's party, the intimacy that Ronald Merrick has forced on him there, and his earlier conversation with Purvis about the political situation at the end of the war, all have contributed to the substance of what Perron writes. But none of this detracts from his objectivity. On the contrary it is because Perron is a historian *and* a man who has had experiences thrust upon him that could only have occurred during the winding-up of the raj that his commentary on Indians and Englishmen is so much to the point: .

> For at least a hundred years India has formed part of England's idea about herself and for the same period India has been forced into a position of being a reflection of that idea. Up to say 1900 the part India played in our idea about ourselves was the part played by anything we possessed which we believed it was right to possess (like a special relationship with God). Since 1900, certainly since 1918, the reverse has obtained. The part played since then by India in the English idea of Englishness has been that of something we feel it does us no credit to have. Our idea about ourselves will now not accommodate any idea about India except the idea of returning it to the Indians in order to prove that we are English and have demonstrably English ideas. All this is quite simply proven and amply demonstrated. But on either side of that arbitrary date (1900) India itself, as itself, that is to say India as not part of our idea of ourselves, has played no part whatsoever in the lives of Englishmen in general (no part that we are conscious of) and those who came out (those for whom India had to play a real part) became detached both from English life and from the English idea of life. Getting rid of India will cause us at home no qualm of conscience because it will be like getting rid of what is no longer reflected in our mirror of ourselves. The sad thing is that whereas in the English mirror there is now no Indian reflection . . . in the Indian mirror the English reflection may be very hard to get rid of, because in the Indian mind English possession has not been an idea but a reality; often a harsh one. The other sad thing is that people like the Laytons may now see nothing at all when looking in their mirror, not even themselves.
>
> *A Division of the Spoils*, 1, i, 2

The reason this account rings true to anyone reading it in its proper setting in the *Quartet* is that the beliefs and ideas it talks about have been fully dramatised in the lives of many of the characters we have met. These include Perron himself, whose historian's objectivity is retrospective and fails to safeguard him from an involvement with Anglo-Indians and their idea of India that is quite incomprehensible, for example, to his dotty Aunt Charlotte back in London. The fundamental fact Perron has grasped is that there is not one India but two. On the one hand there is the idea of India, about which any number of political attitudes can be taken – from the Imperial pride of Wavell and the raj, to the liberal qualms of conscience of Cripps and the Fabian intellectuals. Scott provides ample opportunity for representatives of all these points of view to express them and to act on them; just as, from the other side of the Imperial relationship, he allows both the profound and the trivial differences of opinion among the Muslim, Hindu and Congress politicians to be thoroughly explored in the behaviour of people like Muhammed Kasim, Pandit Baba and the Nawab of Mirat. Perron is not the only character to interpret in an articulate way the Indian situation as he sees it. Rowan, Bronowsky, the Governor (Sir George Malcolm) and several members of Kasim's family all entertain different views about it, and are given innumerable opportunities to disseminate those views: in con-versation, letters, diaries, notebooks, public examinations. The forms in which political sentiments are communicated are immensely varied.

But there is another India, 'India itself, as itself, that is to say India as not part of our idea of ourselves', which makes its presence felt within the pattern of activities that constitutes the plot of the *Quartet*. There is irony in the fact that this India, quite different from the English illusion which sustained a foreign presence in the land for more than two hundred years, is less likely to impinge on the consciousness of the Indians themselves than it is on the English who are leaving, because 'in the Indian mind English possession had not been an idea but a reality'. This is not Scott's major preoccupation, though he handles it very sensitively in his portrayal of the Kasims. What Scott is preoccupied with is the effect the loss of India had on the Anglo-Indian community, on people like the Laytons and the families in whose circles they move in Mayapore, Ranpur and Pankot. The sad thing, he says, is that 'people like the Laytons may now see nothing at all when looking in their mirror, not even themselves'. But he is wrong. His estimate of the Laytons has been less than reliable from the beginning, in spite of his brief affair with Sarah. In responding to them as a type of Anglo-Indian family, with all that goes into the making of such a type, he has failed to discriminate between differences within the type which may be more significant in some cases than the similarities. He came into the novel too late to encounter the distinctly 'different' behaviour of Mabel Layton. But even with Sarah he makes the mistake of supposing that she participates much more fully in the Anglo-Indian solidarity than she really does.

Sarah's history is one of gradual self-liberation from what at first appears to be the ineradicable identity as a pukka miss-sahib that she has inherited from both sides of her family, the Muirs and the Laytons. Because her deep sense of inherited identity has given her a hold on her personality that her prettier but less stable sister, Susan, tragically lacks, she can afford to behave in an unshowily independent way. This makes the memsahibs of Pankot suspicious of her. There is nothing tangible they can point to. Sarah has been a model daughter and a tower of strength to the family during the father's absence. But something is felt to be wrong; and it is Lucy Smalley, the least pukka member of Pankot's female community, who puts her finger on it:

> 'If you ask me,' young Mrs Smalley said – and hesitated because she was never asked and had not been asked now . . . the trouble is she doesn't really take it seriously.' After an appreciable pause Mrs Paynton inquired, 'Take what seriously?'
> 'Any of it,' Mrs Smalley said. 'Us. India. What we're here for. I mean in spite of everything. In spite of her – well, what she was brought up to.'   *The Day of the Scorpion*, I, i, 3

Earlier, when the conversation among the ladies had been dominated by the news from Mayapore, Mrs Smalley said she thought that 'sometimes she was bursting to come out with something, well, critical of us. Just as if she thought it was all our fault.' Or later: '. . . sometimes she looked at me as if I were, well, not a real person.' As the novel unfolds it becomes evident that Sarah's sense of her own reality depends on her awareness of the unreality of the world the British have built around themselves. And this is the world in which, for many years now, she herself has lived. It also becomes evident that she has acquired some of her sense of personal reality, as distinct from the fabricated reality of the English presence in India, from her great aunt Mabel. Sarah was on particularly friendly terms with her, back in England during her schooldays. She still feels deeply about her in spite of Mabel's isolation up at Rose Cottage, away from the rest of the family. It was Mabel who, after her second husband's death, when she was already in semi-retirement from the English community, refused to contribute anything to the General Dyer fund (set up to show approval of his decisive action at Amritsar in 1919). Instead she donated the equivalent amount to a fund for the Indian widows and orphans created by the massacre.

Sarah has inherited some of her great-aunt's independence of mind and, what goes with it, her disposition to place moral considerations above considerations of colour and race. It is this combination of independence and 'colour blindness' that draws her to Lady Manners and Parvati, and so to the Bibighar affair. The disengagement from her Anglo-Indian 'character' eventually expresses itself in a 'casting out of herself of all her inheritance and [being] left in possession – as it were of a relic – of a shell whose emptiness was the proof for future generations of where the fault had lain and why there could have been no other end, even for her'. Buried deep in her, though, is something more than the mere emptiness she discovers here. This is brought out in an exchange of words with Ronald Merrick when they meet at Susan's wedding. Merrick tells her that when he saw her at first, sitting in a taxi, she reminded him of Daphne Manners. And since she is being escorted in Mirat by Ahmed Kasim, Merrick says that in the taxi 'I think there was a sort of fantasy in my mind of Hari and Daphne being about to come together again . . . You sat there in the front seat, shading your eyes – and that was like her. She had a way of standing, peering at things a long way off, with just that gesture. And at the end of the journey, the guest house, and Ahmed there, well – waiting. On the other side of the line.'

No doubt we remember that Merrick had fancied himself in love with Daphne Manners. Now he is drawing as close as he can to the only available female member of another impeccably

pukka English family. He has his reasons for imposing the image
of Daphne Manners on the person of Sarah Layton. But the
impression this little episode makes on the reader, who is not yet
aware of how complex Merrick's personality and ambitions are,
is a vivid one. It coexists with her respect for her aunt Mabel, and
with her visit to Lady Manners' houseboat at Srinagar, to
produce a picture of Sarah as a second Daphne. She becomes
another young girl who is prepared to step over on to the other
side of the line of which Merrick is fond of speaking; to enter the
'other India' into which Kumar has already descended and from
which, perhaps, Ahmed is at this very moment beckoning.
Sarah's attraction to Ahmed, though it never flowers into the
intimacy of a consciously shared relationship, is a very important
aspect of the events that follow.

   As Beloff points out, the fundamental barrier between English
and Indian was the barrier of colour. And as Scott has shown in
some of his earlier novels, with their Eurasian preoccupations
and romantic attachments between young men and women of
different colour, the ultimate test of the colour bar was the
willingness or otherwise of men and women, particularly women,
to transgress it in the cultivation of sexual relationships. 'Even
when social relationships were a little loosened the reluctance to
contemplate the sexual involvement of British women and
Indian men remained a rooted one.' (Beloff) But what Daphne
did in fact, and Sarah was to do in her heart and mind, was to
expose this artificial reluctance to the test of their sexual
demands. In their different ways they both opened their
personalities to an India that lay far beneath the impotent,
though, for the time being, imposing illusions which the British
had constructed out of their own collective imagination.

   Ironically the very first description of the British-Indian
relationship, on the first page of *The Jewel in the Crown*, has at its
centre a metaphor of sexual union. The affair that began on the
evening of 9 August 1942, in Mayapore, we are told, ended with
'the spectacle of two nations in violent opposition, not for the first
time nor as yet for the last because they were then still locked in
an imperial embrace of such long standing and subtlety it was no
longer possible for them to know whether they hated or loved one
another, or what it was that held them together and seemed to
have confused the image of their separate destinies'. In fact the

'imperial embrace' was sterile, a brutal rape rather than a gradual process of mutual comprehension. As Beloff puts it, 'Paul Scott does convey the full tragic significance of the combination between a sense of duty and a sense of permanent alienation from those to whom the duty was owed that is at the heart of the matter.' This fundamental fact about the relationship between English and Indians, however, is modified in some circumstances and in some places. The Princely States, ultimately subject to the British Crown, though in many important respects having the character of autonomous dominions covering a third of the land mass of India, are one example of such a modification – which the scenes at Mirat do much to illuminate. But by far the most important modifications are those involving private relationships between individuals. These extend from Lady Manners' friendship with Lili Chatterjee to the 'illicit' affairs between people like Hari Kumar and Daphne Manners. The second Part of *The Jewel in the Crown* emblematises the complex possibilities of such relationships in the two main locations in which the events of the novel take place – the MacGregor House and the Bibighar Gardens.

We have seen that in several of the novels Scott was writing shortly before the *Quartet* relationships between people were mirrored in relationships between the places in which they met. In *The Chinese Love Pavilion* the position of the oriental pavilion (facing the merchant's house, with the garden of madness stretching between) provided an exotic milieu for the narrative and symbolised much of the passionate activity that was enacted inside it. The same was true of the cage, the island and the encircling estate at Jundapur, with its legend of Krishna's encounter with the prince and the princess, that appeared in some of the central scenes of *The Birds of Paradise*. Here again, in *The Jewel in the Crown*, the event on which so much of the activity of the rest of the *Quartet* depends – the rape of Daphne Manners – occurs in and near places that have a symbolic relation to each other, and whose symbolic ambiance is brought out by the author in a vivid description of their histories.

'Next, there is the image of a garden: not the Bibighar Garden but the garden of the MacGregor House . . .' So, at the opening of Daphne's story, the two most important places that belong to it are linked in the same sentence. Like the Bibighar, the garden here at the MacGregor House is steeped in the green shadows of a rank and overgrown vegetation. In the shadows 'there are dark blue veils, the indigo dreams of plants fallen asleep, and odours of sweet and necessary decay, numerous places layered with the cast-off fruit of other years softened into compost, feeding the living roots that lie under the garden massively, in hungry immobility'. The passing of the years has done nothing to obscure the essential history and character of the place. Quite the contrary. The years seem to have nourished what has happened in the past and brought it alive into the present scene. The particular features of the vegetation, too, may be interpreted as emblems of past and present, since we are told that some of the bushes of white and red bougainvillaea which surround the lawn are hybrids 'and have branches that bear sprays of both colours'. Although in a later passage we are told that MacGregor and Bibighar are 'the place of the white and the place of the black', here, it seems, a joining of the two has at one time taken place, and might take place again when the 'living roots' that lie in 'hungry immobility' under the garden are fed by a new passion between English and Indian.

At first the history of the MacGregor House and the history of the Bibighar seem straightforward, admitting only one interpretation. The original building where the MacGregor House now stands, we are told, was created in the late eighteenth century by an Indian prince. He had conceived a passion for a singer of classical music, and had built her a house where he could visit her in the morning and the evening so that she could sing to him 'the same song perhaps that the girl is singing now' – which is a *raga*, 'the song of a young bride saying goodbye to her parents before setting out on the journey to her new home far away'. When the singer died the prince died also, of a broken heart, and the house fell into decay. The prince's son, who despised his father for his unconsummated attachment to the singer, left the house in ruins and built another house, the Bibighar, nearby. Here he kept his courtesans, until his misgovernment of the State resulted in its annexation by the British. After this the ruined house of the singer was rebuilt by a Scottish merchant called MacGregor, and the Bibighar was burned to the ground because, MacGregor said, 'it had been an abomination'. Now the gardens of both houses are believed to be haunted. Though the archway that leads from the

Bibighar to the road is open for people to enter, 'Children believe that it is haunted'. And the verandah of the MacGregor House is visited from time to time by the ghost of MacGregor's young wife, murdered with her dead baby in her arms by treacherous sepoys during the Mutiny of 1857–58.

The MacGregor House, then, is built on the site of a delicate romance pregnant with mystery and legend, overlaid with the ornate pretensions of a philistine and a puritan, then overlaid again by a tale of violence, murder and ghostly visitations. The Bibighar is the site of a private brothel razed to the ground and visited now by summer picnickers, perennial ghosts, and occasional lovers grateful for the shrubbery and creepers that beckon from the side of the old bridge and the road into Mayapore.

That is the story as we first hear it at the beginning of Part Two of *The Jewel in the Crown*. Lili Chatterjee, who tells the first part of Daphne Manners' story, does not contradict it. But the second part of the story is told by Sister Ludmila, who knows more about its real history and topography than any of the other narrators do. She has been in closer contact, too, with Daphne and Hari, who used to meet at her sanctuary, where the poor and destitute of Mayapore came to receive free medical treatment.

Sister Ludmila tells a different version of the MacGregor story. She believes that the merchant burned down Bibighar, not because it was an abomination, but because he had fallen in love with an Indian girl and had lost her to a boy whose skin was the same colour as her own. There are two versions of this story, she explains. The first says that when MacGregor discovered the Indian girl and her lover in the Bibighar he destroyed it in a fit of jealous rage. The second says that he went to Calcutta to marry an English woman, having prepared the Bibighar for his Indian mistress to live in. When he returned and found she had stolen away with her lover, he burned the Bibighar to the ground. In some renderings of this version the Indian lovers perished in the flames, and may be the ghosts who are rumoured to haunt the present-day gardens. According to these versions the ghost of Janet MacGregor does not visit the MacGregor House to look for her dead child, but to warn that the house is not a good place for people with white skins to live in.

The history suggests that the MacGregor House and the

Bibighar Gardens are closely connected by the passions of those
who have inhabited them in the past. But it also suggests that the
connection has always issued in violence, and, finally,
separation – especially when the lovers have tried to cross the
seemingly impregnable barrier of race. An invisible river runs
between the two places. 'No bridge was ever thrown across it. To
get from one to the other you could not cross by a bridge but had
to take your courage in your hands and enter the flood and let
yourself be taken with it, lead where it may.' As with Brian Saxby
and Tom Brent, echoing Stein's opinion about Jim, Sister
Ludmila is commending Daphne's decision to immerse herself in
'the destructive element'. That is what the history of the two
houses, and her own sense of duty, impel her to do.

   The rape in the Bibighar Gardens destroys whatever might
have evolved from the consummation of Daphne's love of Hari
Kumar. Daphne cannot provide Hari with an impeccable alibi
for the time at which the assault took place, because Hari was
there, and had been making love with her immediately before the
Indians arrived. No British court of law could have been
expected to believe that the penetration of a white girl by a
coloured man was anything other than rape. But because
Daphne finds other ways of protecting Hari from the accusation
of rape, Merrick has to separate him from her by bringing
forward the charge of 'association' with known political radicals.
Therefore Kumar languishes in gaol during the first three
volumes of the *Quartet*, remaining ignorant of the fact that
Daphne has died giving birth to Parvati, who is probably his
child. The five-year span of the *Quartet* does not allow Parvati
herself to develop a character, or form relationships which might
impose some posthumous value on what was otherwise the tragic
issue of Hari's and Daphne's love.

   The colour issue is discussed by many of the characters, but
clearly, in view of the role she plays, Daphne's opinions about it
are of paramount importance. The first thing Daphne notices
when she admits to herself that she is in love with Hari is how
much larger the world has grown. In a way this is true in a literal
sense, because it opens up areas of the city of Mayapore with
which few other members of the white community are familiar. It
is even more true in another sense, which one hesitates to call
psychological or moral, but which contains elements of both of

these qualities. The truth of it dawns on Daphne when she notices the characteristic expression on the faces of the English. It is one of strain – 'the strain of pretending that the world was this small. Hateful. Ingrown. About to explode like powder compressed ready for firing.' It is about to explode because of the disappearance of that sense of mission and service and identification with Indian purposes that Perron was to write about in his notebooks. The relationship with India is now exposed as one based on 'violation':

> Perhaps at one time there was a moral as well as a physical force at work. But the moral thing had gone sour. Has gone sour. Our faces reflect the sourness. The women look worse than the men because consciousness of physical superiority is unnatural to us. A white man in India can feel physically superior without unsexing himself. But what happens to a woman if she tells herself that ninety-nine per cent of the men she sees are not men at all, but creatures of an inferior species whose colour is their main distinguishing mark? What happens when you unsex a nation, treat it like a nation of eunuchs? Because that's what we've done isn't it?
>
> *The Jewel in the Crown*, 7

This is an exemplification of Beloff's point, and that of many historians of the post-Mutiny phase of the raj, that the breakdown of trust between the two races was severely exacerbated by the conduct of the memsahibs. The result was that 'There's dishonesty on both sides because the moral issue has gone sour on them as well as on us . . . It's our fault it's dead because it was our responsibility to widen it, but we narrowed it down by never suiting actions to words.'

So far Daphne's insight into the truth of the matter is no sharper than that of other well-meaning English people and Indians who have reflected seriously on it. These would include Guy Perron and Sarah Layton and also, in this first volume, Edwina Crane, Lili Chatterjee, and Robin White, the Deputy Commissioner at Mayapore. In *The Towers of Silence* they would include even a minor character like Isabel Rankin, a stalwart supporter of the raj ideal. All of these people, with varying degrees of fervour and conviction, accuse the British of lack of wisdom in postponing Independence indefinitely. Each of them also, perhaps with the exception of Isabel, honestly confronts the fact that the reasons for this have to do fundamentally with the colour of the skin. Lili Chatterjee refers to the fact that 'behind all that pretence there was a fear and dislike between us that was rooted in the question of the colour of the skin'. More movingly, after her experience on the road from Dibrapur, Edwina Crane recognises that 'the tragedy is that between us there is this little matter of the colour of the skin, which gets in the way of our seeing through each other's feelings and seeing into each other's hearts. Because if we saw through *them*, into *them*, then we should know. And what we should know is that a promise is a promise and will be fulfilled.' It is on the same note that Daphne concludes her speculations on the English-Indian relationship, before she undergoes the doubly traumatic experience at the Bibighar. Those actions, those words, 'We never suited them because . . . that old primitive savage instinct to attack and destroy what we didn't understand because it looked different always got the upper hand. And God knows how many centuries you have to go back to trace to its source their apparent fear of skins paler than their own . . .'

It is one of the ironies of the situation at the Bibighar that Daphne's behaviour after the assault is entirely consistent with the point she makes here about *other people's* belief in the superiority of white skin to brown. The attack on her exemplifies what she has said about the primitive instinct to destroy or defile anything that is different: nothing could have been more obviously different than the colour of Daphne's skin as compared with that of her Indian assailants. But what follows from the assault – Daphne's own insistence on taking control of the situation – is an even more convincing manifestation of the truth of what she had said. Even in her panic, she admits, 'there was this assumption of superiority, of privilege, of believing I knew what was best for both of us, because the colour of my skin automatically put me on the side of those who never told a lie'. That, also, was Adela Quested's strength in the Marabar Caves in *A Passage to India*: her change of mind about what happened in the cave was the root cause of the profound mistrust in which, had she continued to live in India, she would always have been held. In *The Jewel in the Crown*, Daphne's lie is intended to work to Hari's, the Indian's, advantage. But it is only half successful because she has underestimated Merrick's hatred of Hari, his burning sense of having been humiliated by Daphne's preference for Hari over himself.

Daphne exposes the British idea of justice in India, the idea that still provides them with the illusion of moral superiority and therefore the dispensation to rule. She compares it with a robot. 'We've created a blundering judicial robot', she says. 'We can't stop it working. It works for us even when we least want it to. We created it to prove how fair, how civilised we are. But it is a white robot and it can't distinguish between love and rape. It only understands physical connection and only understands it as a crime because it only exists to punish crime.' When she goes on to wonder what would happen if someone came along and, by error or good judgement, fixed into it 'a special circuit with the object of making it impartial and colour blind' she looks forward, without knowing it, to what she herself is to achieve during the inquiry that follows Hari's arrest. Then she is given the opportunity, through the questions Judge Menen puts to her, of creating that 'special circuit'. She is able to go to the heart of the judicial mechanism, to expose it for what it is, 'by imposing an impossible task on it – the task of *understanding* the justice of what it was doing, and of proving that its own justice was the equal or the superior of mine'. She is able to do this by making two claims: that the youths who raped her could have been white youths with blacked faces; and that one of them was circumcised, and must therefore have been a Muslim – i.e. not one of the five Hindu suspects who were arrested with Hari. These are 'facts' the robot is not equipped to deal with. The customary assumptions about relations between black and white, which the Bibighar case seemed to endorse so completely, are thrown into confusion as the racial identities of the parties concerned are shown to be ambiguous – resistant to categories of black and white on the basis of which the judicial machine is programmed to function.

No one inside the English community can bring himself to disbelieve in the judicial system entirely, even when (like Robin White or Nigel Rowan) he has the soundest liberal credentials, backed up by considerable experience of India and Indians. That is why when Daphne's baby is born she is given into the protection of Lady Manners, who lives now quite outside the English circle and the raj. When Lady Manners dies the child will be brought up by her Indian friend Lili Chatterjee. She will grow up in an Anglo-Indian aristocracy which is colour-blind, and which is untouched by the racial bitterness which the British move towards Independence and the Indian move towards partition are formenting at the heart of the political system.

It is of great symbolic importance that Sarah Layton is the only English person in the *Quartet* to visit Lady Manners and see the baby. As Barbie Batchelor suggests to her, it is strange how closely involved Sarah has become, in a roundabout way, in the Bibighar affair – although it occurred more than two years before she arrived in Pankot, and most nearly concerned two people whom she had never met and would never meet. For not only has Sarah visited Lady Manners. She has also become closely involved with Ronald Merrick, the 'third party' to the affair, whose relationship with her sister Susan involves Sarah closely in all that is most wilfully destructive of the Anglo-Indian 'embrace'.

To grasp the significance of Ronald Merrick's involvement with the Laytons it is necessary to understand what exactly was the nature of his contact with Hari Kumar after the arrest in August 1942. This remains shrouded in mystery throughout *The Jewel in the Crown*, which doesn't explain what happened to Hari after the arrest. Instead, it moves away from his present circumstances and gives an account of his parents' history and his childhood. This it does by way of a bridge-passage brought forward to a date several years after Independence. During 'An Evening at the Club', Lili Chatterjee and Mr Srinivasan, the lawyer, touch only lightly on the Bibighar case in their discussion of the politics of partition. Thereafter the narrative returns to the events in Mayapore in August 1942, but from the civil and military point of view, in letters, memoirs and depositions from those who played a political part of some kind in the events of that time. In the deposition of an Indian journalist called Vidyasagar (first encountered in *The Alien Sky*) we are given one, possibly biased, account of the ill-treatment Kumar received at Merrick's hands. Then the narrative moves back in time again, and offers us the full story of Hari's relationship with Daphne Manners, and its premature end at Bibighar. A complete record of what happened between Kumar and Merrick has to wait until we are half-way through *The Day of the Scorpion*. There Hari tells the story in his own words in a way that seems to convince Rowan (who is conducting Hari's examination) and certainly convinces Lady Manners (who has been allowed to overhear the examination from the secrecy of an adjoining room) that Merrick's account is utterly untrue.

Merrick plays such an important part in the *Quartet* that it is worthwhile following his career as it is described in the first two volumes, before we come to the exposé of his character produced by Hari during Rowan's examination. He is the only character who plays a prominent part in all four novels. And it is his relationship with Sarah Layton, built on the sub-structure of Daphne's relationship with Hari Kumar, that gives the *Quartet* its basic shape, so far as the plot is concerned.

We hear about Merrick's efficient handling of the riots in Mayapore *en passant* during the first Part of *The Jewel*, which is devoted to the story of Edwina Crane. Later Brigadier Reid and Robin White both pass comment on him in his capacity as Divisional Superintendent of Police. But our first glimpse of him face to face, as it were, is in a letter Daphne writes to Lady Manners from Mayapore when she has been staying there at the MacGregor House for a little more than six months. Ronald Merrick has invited her to dinner at his bunglow and, after showing her around the house, has made her a proposal of marriage. She has not been able to accept his proposal. But he has made it in such a way that they are able to remain on friendly terms for some time afterwards. Daphne doesn't find it easy to explain what it is about Ronald Merrick that seems so unsatisfactory. He is very handsome, he has a formidable reputation for doing his job well, and a girl like Daphne would not be put off by his humble background, his having risen through the ranks of the Indian Civil Service. 'People don't like you much', she ponders, 'but you're fundamentally *kind*.' Nevertheless she admits to herself that 'there was and still is . . . a distinct reservation (from my point of view) that must be something to do with what I feel is the lack of *real* candour between him and whoever he's dealing with. I never feel quite *natural* when I'm with him, but can never be sure whether it's my fault or his.'

Daphne is responding to an aspect of Merrick that is sensed by almost every other person in the novel – with the exception of Susan Layton, the defects of whose personality fatally disequip

her from understanding or even noticing this quality in the man
who eventually becomes her husband. Later we are to discover
how it relates to other traits of personality which Daphne either
dismisses or hopelessly misunderstands. She mentions the repro-
ductions of Henry Moore drawings of underground figures
during the blitz that decorate the rooms of his living room; and
the scented soap (Coty Chypre) in the closet ('The soap in his
own bathroom was Lifebuoy, so don't jump to the wrong
conclusion!'); and she comments, in an inappropriately light-
hearted way, that 'He must be a wizard at interrogation! That's
not fair. But you know what I mean.' Much of Merrick's real
personality is present in these brief, sidelong glimpses, but, like
Daphne, we probably fail to take them sufficiently into account.

It is greatly to Scott's credit that, before Merrick comes to the
forefront of the story, we have received such a vivid impression of
the kind of man he is and the awkward impact he makes on the
people around him. These impressions have to be tested against
the appalling allegations Hari Kumar makes to Nigel Rowan;
against what he himself tells Sarah Layton from his hospital bed
in Calcutta about his relationship with Teddie Bingham; against
his behaviour at Pankot, when Guy Perron discovers how he has
been abusing his position as a lieutenant-colonel, later colonel, in
Intelligence; and, lastly, against what we gradually discover
about his relationship with Susan and his houseboys in the
bungalow at Ranpur.

Merrick is the last in a long line of Scott's characters who take a
sadistic delight in totally dominating and humiliating those
whom they select as their victims. The element of secrecy and
danger invloved in playing this 'game' is a necessary part of it,
and Merrick enjoys pushing a situation to its limits – where
exposure of himself is gambled against the total disintegration of
his victim's character and, on occasion, his death. In the past
such characters have included Dwight MacKendrick in *The Alien
Sky*, Brian Saxby in *The Chinese Love Pavilion*, and Edward
Thornhill's uncle James in *The Corrida at San Felíu*. (There is also
the hero of Thornhill's short story 'The Leopard Mountain', who
is modelled on Uncle James and who behaves in a similarly
manic-depressive way.) All these characters have 'lists' of the
victims they intend to humiliate, even to murder (Saxby murders
the Malayan collaborators on his lists; and it is because Teena

Chang's name is also on the list that Brent's manhunt for Saxby
becomes so urgently personal a matter). It is significant that
Merrick is also described as making out lists. When Guy Perron
and Nigel Rowan are travelling with Merrick on the train to
Pankot, Rowan wants to know why Merrick will not allow
Colonel Layton to see his old havildar, Karim Muzzafir Khan,
who has been detained for questioning on suspicion of treason:

> 'What's so special about Havildar Karim Muzzafir Khan that
> Delhi sends a half-colonel all the way to Pankot to take
> statements?'
> 'Oh that's easy [Perron replies]. The havildar was special
> business because Merrick chose him.'
> 'You mean as an example?'
> 'I mean he was a chosen one. It's part of the technique of the
> self-invented man. Merrick looks round, his eye lights on
> someone, and he says, Right, I want *him*. Why else do you
> think I'm here? I'm a chosen one. I expect Coomer was.'
>
> *A Division of the Spoils*, i, ii, 6

The upshot of this peculiarity of Merrick's personality we witness
at Pankot where we follow the fortunes of Muzzafir Khan (he
commits suicide after being questioned by Merrick: 'He must be
a wizard at interrogation' – Sarah) and a wretched young private
called Pinky, whose latent homosexuality is encouraged and
exposed as a side-effect of one of Merrick's more ambitious
schemes. But it is the way Kumar was chosen and what happened
to him that concerns us now, because this is the first clear
evidence of Merrick's perverse attitude to other human beings. It
is also important because it magnifies – in its deviant sexuality, its
masochism, its sadism, and its arrogance – some of the real facts of
the Anglo-Indian relationship.

The facts about Kumar's physical punishment are gone into in
some detail. All that needs to be said about them here is that they
include Kumar's being stripped naked, tied to a trestle, and
beaten with a cane to the point at which he almost loses
consciousness. Afterwards Merrick tries to get him to ejaculate by
sexually abusing him. And all the time he is talking without
pause about the rape of Daphne Manners. This violent beating
and sexual assault is interrupted by a long harangue by Merrick

about what he calls 'the situation', by which he means the
coming together of himself and Kumar in this totally appropriate
circumstance. Only in such a 'situation', Merrick believes, can
they 'enact' the real relationship between them, which is the real
relationship not only between two individuals but between two
nations, the English and the Indian:

> . . . He said for the moment we were mere symbols. He said
> we'd never understand each other if we were going to be
> content with that. It wasn't enough to say he was English and I
> was Indian, that he was a ruler and I was one of the ruled. We
> had to find out what that meant. He said people talked of an
> ideal relationship between his kind and my kind. They called it
> comradeship. But they never said anything about the con-
> tempt on his side and the fear on mine that was basic, and came
> before any comradely feeling. He said we had to find out about
> that too, we had to enact the situation as it really was, and in a
> way that would mean neither of us ever forgetting it or being
> tempted to pretend it didn't exist, or was something
> else. . . . He said the true corruption of the English is their
> pretence that they have not contempt for us, and our real
> degradation is our pretence of equality. He said if we could
> understand the truth there might be a chance for us. There
> might be some sense then in talking about his kind's obli-
> gations to my kind. The last phase could show the possibilities.
>
> *The Day of the Scorpion*, II, i, 2

Merrick's view of the world is one that revolves around the twin
poles of envy and contempt. Everything else is deception,
certainly everything the Laytons believed in when they used
words like 'service' and 'loyalty' to define their attitudes towards
the Indians. Whilst Sarah has been moving towards a new and
less self-deceiving relationship with India than the rest of the
Laytons (except great-aunt Mabel, perhaps) have acquired;
Merrick has all along despised the 'Layton' view of India as
'amateur' and hypocritical, either ignorant of or not daring to
acknowledge the real bonds of envy and contempt that are
symbolised in his treatment of Kumar. That is the main reason
why Sarah refers to him as 'our dark side', 'the arcane side' of the
English colonial temperament. 'You reveal something that is sad

about us', she says, 'as if out here we had built a mansion without doors and windows, with no way in and no way out.' She senses this in Merrick although at this stage she has no idea of what he has done to Hari, and therefore of what kind of man he really is.

Hari Kumar sums up the 'situation' Merrick described in the prison, in the following terms: (He said you couldn't buck this issue, . . . that relationships between people were based on contempt, not love, and that contempt was the prime human emotion because no human being was ever going to believe all human beings were born equal. If there was an emotion almost as strong as contempt it was envy. He said a man's personality existed at the point of equilibrium between the degree of his envy and the degree of his contempt.') That is the nearest Merrick comes to providing a rationale of his conduct. It is an intensely self-deceived one, because although he may really believe human beings live in the loveless cage of envy and contempt into which he has locked himself, he refuses to admit that in the relationship between himself and Kumar *his* is the envious role. He is envious of Hari's association with Daphne, which, of course, he refuses to accept at its true valuation. But he is also envious of the fact that, take away his brown skin, and Hari Kumar becomes Harry Coomer. As such, he is much more the pukka English gentleman than Merrick can ever be. Therefore what Merrick is beating and humiliating in Kumar is not only the envious Indian for whom he feels contempt, but the contemptuous English public school boy for whose class, accent and perfect manners he feels the deepest, though un-self-acknowledged, envy.

From his hospital bed in Calcutta, Merrick is still mouthing his contempt for Teddie Bingham's 'amateur' view of the war and his sentimental attitude towards his old Indian unit, the 'Muzzy Guides'. But Sarah, who is listening to his account of Teddie's death, and Merrick's heroic effort to save him, is not convinced. Instead of what Merrick is showing her, she sees 'a man who was in love with those legends, that way of life, all those things that from a distance seemed to distinguish people like us from people of his own kind, people he knew better. I see a man still in love with them but who has chosen to live outside in the cold because he couldn't get in to warm his hands at this hearth with its dying fire.' Sarah reflects on these matters at a time when she is moving from the India she believes Merrick would have liked to enter.

She is detaching herself from the shell of an illusory India of regimental trophies, family heirlooms, sentiments about the Muzzy Guides, and all the rest. But she is unlikely to enter the nihilistic universe out of which Merrick is trying to crawl towards the world that is represented by all that she is casting aside. Gradually she is coming to terms with another India, one that Merrick's Intelligence has no knowledge of, because it lies far beneath the political and racial ambitions in which he has tried to forge his character and against which he still dramatises his brittle personality.

Perron's view of Ronald Merrick is that 'He's the man who comes too late and invents himself to make up for it', and there is a great deal of truth in this comment. But it is the old Russian Count, Bronowsky, who understands him most thoroughly:

> 'He is one of your hollow men. The outer casing is almost perfect and he carried it off almost to perfection. But, of course, it is a casing he has designed. This loss he has sustained – the left arm – even this fits. If he regrets the loss, presently he will see that he has lost nothing or anyway gained more in compensation. What an interesting thought. I am tempted to say that had he not suffered the loss he might one day have been forced to invent it.'
>
> Rowan smiled. 'To the extent of removing part of a limb?'
> Bronowsky laughed.
> 'But absolutely!'
> For a while he gazed at Rowan and then said sedately: 'I speak metaphorically, naturally.'
>
> *A Division of the Spoils*, 1, ii, 4

After his death, Bronowsky sees the connection between the hollowness and the homosexuality, the sado-masochism, the sense of social inferiority and 'the grinding defensive belief in his racial superiority' that Merrick has experienced. His affair with the houseboy, Aziz (Bronowsky believes), was the first physical homosexual relationship he had had and the peace he discovered after it could not hide from him the connections between these different aspects of his personality. But such a recognition brought with it intimations of the insufficiency of the outlook on life which had dictated the character of all his actions until now. From this moment on his willingness to perform the role of victim rather than persecutor becomes uppermost in his mind. The facet of his character that mocked at the challenge of the thrown stone, at the woman on the station platform, at the mysterious marks on the doors and walls of his encampment, and at the appearance of symbolic bicycles in his vicinity (he had planted Daphne's bicycle near Hari's house when he was trying to implicate him in the Bibighar rape) grew under his recognition that, as Independence approached, so did his death – no doubt spelt out on the list of some equivalent Hindu fanatic on the other side of the racial boundary. And so he meets his death at the hands of one of Bronowsky's 'dark young men of random destiny and private passion'. As the old Count puts it: 'I am sure that finally . . . he sought the occasion of his own death and that he grew impatient for it . . . He wanted what happened to happen.'

As the facts emerge from a bland report in the newspapers that Merrick died as a result of injuries sustained in a riding accident, and we discover the bloodbath in which he actually met his violent end, the appropriateness of that end, its inevitability, is difficult to ignore. With his strange mixture of perversity and heroism, romantic ambition and sadistic malice, all gradually emerging from the original picture of an efficient Superintendent of Police doing his job well in difficult circumstances, Merrick is surely one of the most fully realised characters in contemporary fiction. At the opposite end of the novel's moral spectrum from the one occupied by Sarah Layton, he makes at least as strong an impression as she does, and amply fills his position in the complex narrative Scott has built around the fortunes of them both.

Merrick's official view of the world is one that insist on the necessity of boundaries. Where boundaries do not exist in fact, as Teddie Bingham believes they do ('The line's already there, isn't it? We don't have to draw it' – the pukka point of view), it is the duty of each individual to draw attention to distinctions in human society and behaviour which would otherwise remain ambiguous, muddled, undisciplined. The trouble with Daphne Manners, according to Merrick, was that she resented what she considered the arbitrary distinctions that had been made between English and Indian. She wasn't able to make the distinction for herself. At the same time she refused to observe the distinctions the English community at large had created. She didn't see why a line had to be drawn:

But it's essential, isn't it? You have to draw the line. Well, it's
arbitrary. Nine times out of ten perhaps you need to draw it in
the wrong place. But you need it there, you need to be able to
say: There's the line. This side of it is right. That side is wrong.
Then you have your moral terms of reference. Then you can
act. You can feel committed. You can be involved. Your life
takes on something like a shape. It has a form. Purpose as well,
maybe. You know who you are when you wake up in the
morning.   *The Day of the Scorpion*, i, iii, 4

Merrick is telling this to Sarah, the person to whom above all
others it cannot be said to apply. The almost frenetic urgency
with which he speaks is not easy to explain at this stage in the
narrative. It issues from the need he feels to depress those deep
impulses of his personality which we are beginning to realise force
him to transgress, amorally and violently, the limits to which he
pretends to attach so much importance. Ultimately, for Merrick,
the lines he draws create temptations to press beyond them,
which must eventually result in his disgrace or death. That is the
real reason he insists on boundaries. Without boundaries chaos
would be the essential principle of life. With them, he can *create*
the chaos, the damage, the destruction that is the true ruling
impulse, the subconscious purpose of his existence.

The view of life to which Merrick says he attaches such
importance is ceasing to matter to Sarah Layton, for the reasons
given by Barbie Batchelor after Sarah's return from Calcutta.
She understands how Sarah might feel that she has 'no clearly
defined world to inhabit, but one poised between the old for
which she had been prepared, but which seemed to be dying, and
the new for which she had not been prepared at all'; 'all the
patterns to which she had been trained to conform were fading,
and she was already conscious just from chance or casual
encounter of the gulf between herself and the person she would
have been if she had never come back to India: the kind of person
she "really was".' The difficulty of her entry into the real India is
the same difficulty that Daphne Manners experienced, and
overcame by an act of real courage. According to Sister Ludmila,
Daphne did not divide conduct into parts: 'She was attempting
always a wholeness. When there is a wholeness there are no
causes. Only there is living. The contribution of the whole of

one's life, the whole of one's resources, to the world at large.'

Sarah is never brought to this final test. After her father's homecoming and Susan's second marriage she decides to leave her family and discover her identity outside the boundaries of the raj, in an Independent India or elsewhere – in England, perhaps. We leave her among the dead and the dying on a train halted between stations at Mirat and Ranpur. Her last thoughts are of Ahmed – as Edwina Crane's were, presumably, of Mr Chaudhuri. She does not see him as another Hari Kumar, with herself playing the part of Daphne Manners. But there is some sort of connection between the two: 'Ahmed and I weren't in love. But we loved one another. We recognised in each other the compulsion to break away from what I can only call a *received* life.' Sarah disappears from the story with the break half-completed, and the man to whom (it has been suggested) she might have turned in order to complete it, slaughtered without sense or reason during the birth pangs of the new India.

When Sarah first meets Ahmed, at the guest house at Mirat, they spend a lot of their time together out riding. It is an experience she has at this time that provides Sarah with an image of what her new life might be:

> The sun was already hot and the short-lived freshness of early morning already staling. She noted the first phase of that curious phenomenon of the Indian plain, the gradual disap-pearance of the horizon, as if the land were expanding, stretching itself, destroying the illusion that the mind, hand and eye could stake a claim to any part that bore a real relation to the whole. It is always retreating, Sarah told herself, always making off, getting farther and farther away and leaving people and what people have built stranded.
>
> *The Day of the Scorpion*, ii, iii, 2

Sarah is experiencing that enlargement of the world that Daphne also experienced, when she confessed to herself that she had fallen in love with Hari Kumar. But for Sarah this does not offer itself as a joyful experience. The formlessness of the Indian plain, the hostility it shows to those who would stake a claim to any part of it which 'bore a real relation to the whole', is frightening. It

conforms to a picture of India which has always lain behind the
animated foreground of the *Quartet*. One remembers the way
the discussion between Lili Chatterjee and Mr Srinivasan
at the 'English Club' ended, after the inevitable formalities and
the political speculation. Where is young Kumar now?, Lady
Chatterjee wonders. To which the lawyer Srinivasan shrugs:

> Well, it is a vast country. Easy to get lost in. And again the
> sense of immensity (of weight and flatness, and absence of
> orientating features) blankets the mind with an idea of scope so
> limitless that it is deadening. Here, on the ground, nothing is
> likely, everything is possible. Only from the air can one trace
> what looks like a pattern, a design, an abortive, human
> intention.
>
> *The Jewel in the Crown*, IV

One recalls Forster's similar observation, less rhetorically and
more enigmatically expressed: 'Looking back at the great blur of
the last twenty-four hours, no man could say where was the
emotional centre of it, any more than he could locate the heart of
a cloud.' And I think one is inclined to wonder: How has Paul
Scott traced what to him 'looks like a pattern' in his fiction? How
has he evolved a form for it which has managed to 'rein in the
horizon'? How has he produced some of those orientating
features that novels cannot do without, at the same time as he has
done justice to the essential intractability of the Indian landscape, and, perhaps, of the human relationships that are
enacted, and aborted, on its surface?

Many of the characters in the *Quartet* find it difficult to offer a
truthful account of the part they have played in the events
recorded. A good example of such a character is Robin White.
His painstaking attempts to correct the bias of Brigadier Reid's
memoir of the Mayapore disturbances are set down with many
apologies and confessions of self-distrust. Even less satisfactory is
the theory of history he advances to explain these events. For in
relating his theory to what he saw actually happening at the time,
he is back in the world of describable events. 'And when I
attempt to relate the theory to all the events in the lives of all the
people who were connected with the action . . . my mind simply
won't take in the complex of emotions and ambitions and

reactions that led, say, to any one of the simple actions that was part of the general describable pattern.')Perhaps, though, he supposes 'the mind can respond to a sense of a cumulative, impersonal justice?'

This last hope is important. It absolves White, and with him I should suppose his creator, from the charge one might be inclined to make about so much inferior modern writing about history: namely that everything is relative, that a novelist can go on more or less for ever adding account to account and point of view to point of view until it becomes obvious that the truth of an 'affair' can never be known because, ultimately, there is no such thing as 'the truth' about anything, let alone something as complex as the behaviour of human beings, or the evolution of societies, or the relation between one of these things and the other. In the end the novelist simply has to stand back baffled at the immensity of the task before him and the egotism of the ambition that drove him to try to perform it. Or, like Lawrence Durrell in the *Alexandria Quartet*, he can throw out a collection of 'work points' at the end of each member of the *Quartet*, inviting the reader to embark again on the never-ending quest for a complete and comprehensive account which, in the nature of things, he must realise does not exist.

Scott's attitude to his responsibilities as a novelist will not allow him to make these elegant surrenders to the mystery of things. I believe he really does think that what he has told us about the last years of the raj is the truth. Essentially, this is what happened and this is how people responded to what happened. Other people might have responded in different ways. Some did. But all people are different. Here is assembled a large cast of such people, whose collective response to the demise of the raj is in a profound way representative.

I think a clue is given to the shape of the *Quartet*, to the way Scott has accomplished his ambition, in a few words spoken by Sir George Malcolm to Nigel Rowan when they are discussing the Kumar case. Malcolm says that he has his own personal theory of relativity. He often uses it when he is trying to reach a solution to a practical problem which is so awkward and so intricate as to appear insoluble. His theory is that 'although people seldom argued a point but argued round it, they sometimes found a solution to the problem they were evading by going round in ever *increasing* circles and disappearing into the centre of *those*, which, relatively speaking, coincided with the centre of the circle from whose periphery they had evasively spiralled out.' Malcolm, of course, is talking about administrative procedure, and problems which require solutions. Whereas Scott has in mind the articulation of fundamentally true facts about a complex human situation, which does not require a solution but which does require an appropriate form. That form, I would suggest, has a great deal in common with Sir George's appearing and disappearing circles.

What Scott is trying to show us in the *Quartet* is that though novels are constructed out of events, and events occur in time; nevertheless, in a way he did not intend, what Merrick told Hari Kumar about the timelessness of the 'situation' in which they found themselves is fundamentally true; and its truth needs to be built into the shape of the novel. In Scott's case, as in Merrick's, the 'situation' is the relationship between English and Indians. We might be encouraged to generalise from this and say that such a relationship is paradigmatic of all relationships involving geographical displacement, the transformation of human attitudes and institutions in the process of time. It is typical of what happens to human relationships when they run up against the twin barriers of race and class. India between 1942 and 1947, though replete with its peculiar dangers and fascinations, offers itself as a distillation of all that is essential to that kind of situation – a situation incidentally which seems to be one of the almost universal situations of our time. Therefore to write a novel in the conventional way, with a time-scheme that passes from event (*a*) to event (*b*) through to event (*y*) or (*z*), would be to construct an eccentric narrative i.e. a narrative that might or might not exemplify some of the themes in which the author is interested; but which will certainly not contain in itself the reason why these themes, episodes, events, symbols are *necessary*. It will not go further than to present itself as one of several ways in which one of several subjects might be treated. If the story ends with its events uncompleted, then another novel can be written in order to complete them, or to conduct the story to a later stage in its still incomplete progress. For the same reasons the themes of the novel might stay unresolved, or its symbolism remain opaque and resistant to interpretation.

Most novels operate on this level. Rightly so where their subject is merely historical, anecdotal, a slice of life or a tract for the times. But Scott is a very ambitious novelist, and he is trying to do much more than that. Though the surface of his novel is historical, and a great deal of its attractiveness lies in its firm grasp of the details of the period in which it is set – the Anglo-Indian social round, regimental traditions, civil service etiquette, and the ubiquitous bric-à-brac of pictures, songs, drinks and uniforms – at its core it is metaphysical. In other words the historical detail is the outward manifestation of ideas about the world which are felt to be incontrovertible, and which are therefore meshed into the episodes of the story so as to bring out a pattern in the way events develop, relate to one another, form a significant network of interrelated plots.

As so often in the first book of the *Quartet*, Sister Ludmila explains Scott's intentions – whilst apparently talking about something completely different. She is telling the narrator where Hari Kumar was deposited after he was brought into the Sanctuary, unconscious, after an uncharacteristic bout of drinking. (He had just discovered that his English friend, Colin Lindsey, had been deliberately ignoring him since his arrival in India.) Later she saw him washing at the old pump, which has now disappeared, because the Sanctuary has been rebuilt not long after the events recorded in the *Quartet* were completed. The purpose, even the very name, of the Sanctuary have been changed since that time. So how can she or anyone else be expected to identify the pump at which she found Hari washing years and years ago? Well, she says, she can still do so, because in a profound sense the pump, and Hari washing at it, have never passed away. Like the narrator she understands that 'a specific historical event has no definite beginning, no satisfactory end . . .':

It is as if time were telescoped? Is that the right word? As if time were telescoped and space dovetailed? As if Bibighar almost had not happened yet, and yet has happened, so that at once past, present and future are contained in your cupped palm. The route you came, the gateway you entered, the buildings you saw here in the Sanctuary – they are to me in spite of the new fourth building, the same route I took, the same buildings

I returned to when I brought the limp body of young Mr
Coomer back to the Sanctuary.   *The Jewel in the Crown*, III

'It is as if time were telescoped and space dovetailed.' Surely this
is an accurate description of what Scott has achieved in his
Quartet. Events do not succeed one another in a straightforward
linear way, rushing from the past into the future. Instead they
curve around from the future into the past and back into the
present – which is always Bibighar, the assault, the arrival of
Daphne Manners at the MacGregor House and the search for
Hari Kumar by Ronald Merrick. This is the 'situation', or, in the
Governor's word, the 'point' from which circles from other events
involving other people continuously spiral outwards, and disap-
pear through the centres of themselves back to Bibighar and
everything it symbolises about those relationships Scott has
isolated as paradigmatic of the human condition.

    The way the plot keeps coming back to Bibighar, forcing the
characters to discuss it and investigate it, and occasionally
increase our knowledge of what happened in it, will need no
emphasising. The last volume ends with Guy Perron's unsuccessful attempt to find Hari in one of the poor quarters of Ranpur.
Also, I have tried to show how the affair between Daphne
Manners and Hari Kumar contains within itself all the essential
properties of the Anglo-Indian situation. Others who are caught
up in that situation, especially Sarah Layton and Ronald
Merrick, are drawn to it through mixed motives of guilt,
curiosity, necessity, the possibility of learning something.
Merrick's career is interrupted again and again by symbolic
reminders of Bibighar: painted signs, a woman in a saree, those
ubiquitous bicycles. They are the visible reminders, symbols for
him of all that Bibighar means that he carries inside himself.

    The dense texture of the writing, with its rich and suggestively
reiterated imagery, testifies to the feeling of sadness at what has
been destroyed. In particular, the love affair between Hari and
Daphne; in general, that rather different affair between the
English and India – which was not altogether lacking in love.
When he considers it appropriate, Scott is able to produce some
of the sparest and tautest narrative prose of this century. At the
beginning and the end of the *Quartet* his descriptions of the assault
on Edwina Crane and Mr Chaudhuri, and the slaughter of the

Muslims on the train to Ranpur, are startlingly vivid and
succinct. But the variety of Scott's prose should be assessed by
looking not only at these rapid accounts of violent ends, but also
at the comedy of Perron's dealings with the 'Red Shadow'; the
pathetic little episode of Pinky and the psychiatric records at
Pankot; the brutally honest description of Clarke's seduction of
Sarah Layton in Calcutta; even the recording of historical events
through the medium of invented cartoons at the beginning of the
second Book of *A Division of the Spoils*. The surfaces of the novels
are more various than my account of them so far might have
suggested. Nevertheless, it would be true to say, I think, that the
staple of Scott's prose is a slow-moving, hesitant, grammatically
complex and heavily loaded sentence structure which gathers
together fragments of what has already been, more than it
propels forward events that are about to come into being. In this
respect the writing is a perfect mirror of the formal stasis of the
novel, as I have described it above. And it provides ample
opportunity for the subtle deployment of Scott's symbolism as
well as the expression of his essentially elegaic tone.

Some of the symbolism of the *Quartet* – like the painting of *The
Jewel in the Crown*, or the destruction of a scorpion in a ring of fire
on the lawn of the Layton compound – is uncomplicated, though
it is used over and over again to bring out unexpected areas of
relevance. Events in the *Quartet* are often of this kind. Indeed the
central event of the rape in the Bibighar Gardens is a symbolic
occurrence which in a sense absorbs into itself everything else
that happens. But the local symbolism is more likely than not to
attach itself to an object which can be transferred from person to
person, gathering into itself a richer and richer significance as it
does so. Two such objects which play especially important roles
in the narrative, though they have little effect on the plot, are
Sarah Layton's christening shawl, and a volume of poems by the
eighteenth-century Urdu poet 'Gaffur'.

The christening shawl makes its first appearance when Sarah is
persuaded by her sister to ask their great-aunt Mabel, who has
the shawl in her possession, if she will give it to her for the
christening of her baby. The story behind the shawl is that it was
made by an old blind retainer of Mabel's French mother-in-law
(by her first husband). The old lady lived in the tower of a
chateau in the Ile de France. When Mabel visited her many years

ago, and received the present of the lace shawl, she saw that on it was a motif of butterflies: 'They were alive, fluttering above her moving hand.' And the old lace-maker answered that 'her heart bled for the butterflies because they could never fly out of the prison of the lace and make love in the sunshine. She could feel the sunshine on her hands but her hands were nothing but a prison for God's most delicate creatures.'

This is a romantic and suggestive little story. One sees its application, on a 'political' level, to the position of the British in India. (It reminds one of the stuffed birds of paradise in the cage at Jundapur in an earlier novel.) And one takes note of psychological comparisons between the blind old lady, creating beauty out of a simulated death; and several of the characters in the novel, who blindly imprison their most urgent desires in a cage of memory or fantasy or a vacuous simulacrum of the satisfactions to which they aspire.

The accidental way in which Barbie Batchelor acquires the shawl after Mabel's death emphasises the bond that has developed between the two women. And the event that finally sends Barbie mad, when the tonga carrying her and her possessions down the hill from Rose Cottage to Pankot collapses and discharges its load, is rendered very much more vivid and suggestively significant by virtue of the fact that at the time she is wearing the shawl over her head 'like a bridal veil'. When she turns her head it is 'a nest of butterflies'. When she falls into the road, 'Now everything is cool again. The rain falls on the dead butterflies on my face . . .' I don't know that it is possible to explain the power and appropriateness of Barbie's wearing the shawl. It has something to do with the coming together of the past of the half-crazy old lace-maker and the present of the not-yet-quite-crazy old missionary – both of them kindly and charitable souls. The touch of fragile white butterflies on the worn, weatherbeaten old face also plays its part. And I think the fact that Barbie dies listening to the birds wheeling round the towers of silence as they pick the bones of the dead Parsees, reminds us, through the medium of the shawl, of the image of a tower shared by two equally destitute old women – the one blind, the other to all intents and purposes dumb – in whom sight and sound were the basis of their professions.

The poems of Gaffur first make their appearance when Sarah

Layton is looking for a suitable gift to express her family's gratitude to the Nawab of Mirat. Lady Manners tells her of the relationship between the eighteenth-century poet and the present day Nawab – both of whom are members of the Kasim family. The gift of the book by Sarah to the uncle and prospective father-in-law (if Bronowsky's plans succeed) of Ahmed Kasim, then, is the suggestion of Daphne's aunt and Parvati's godmother – a minor consequence, in other words, of the Bibighar affair.

The Nawab is not the only recipient of a volume of Gaffur's poems. Guy Perron receives a similar gift from Count Bronowsky, who has translated the poems – as has Brigadier Reid, in a less contemporary manner. One way or another Gaffur's poems circulate among several of the characters. For example Barbie has several quotations from them by heart.

We are not offered any one complete poem by Gaffur until the very last page of the *Quartet*, when Guy Perron decides to examine his copy on the plane out of Ranpur. Earlier he had been writing to Sarah in the airport lounge, mentally incorporating in his letter a passage from an article by 'Philoctetes' in the *Ranpur Gazette*. Guy has realised that 'Philoctetes' is Hari Kumar. So when he slips the letter to Sarah between the pages of Gaffur's poems, a conjunction of sentiments of the most powerful kind provides Scott's novel with an exemplary epilogue. Kumar's prose recalls his life in England. And this was a Paradise lost, if ever there was one in Paul Scott's fiction. For Kumar's transplantation to India was the inevitable prelude to his tragedy:

> I walk [he writes], thinking of another place, of seemingly long endless summers and the shade of different kinds of trees; and then of winters when the branches of the trees were bare, so bare that, recalling them now, it seems inconceivable to me that I looked at them and did not think of the summer just gone, and the spring soon to come, as illusions, as dreams, never fulfilled, never to be fulfilled.
>
> *A Division of the Spoils*, II, iv

Gaffur's poem emphasises the inevitability of loss and the heartbreaking illusoriness of dreams. For Kumar, England. For the Laytons and the Muirs, India. But the poem also circles back on its own sentiments, and gathers together the experiences which have been lost in a formal structure that will not let them go – repeating them over and over again for as long as anyone is there to hear the poem; or, in other places, at other times, for as long as anyone is there to read the novel in which it is embedded:

> Fleeting moments: these are held a long time in the eye,
> The blind eye of the ageing poet,
> So that even you, Gaffur, can imagine
> In this darkening landscape
> The bowman lovingly choosing his arrow,
> The hawk outpacing the cheetah,
> (The fountain splashing lazily in the courtyard),
> The girl running with the deer.
>
> *A Division of the Spoils*, II, vi, coda

Bronowsky is clearly the Arthur Waley of the court of Mirat. But Paul Scott has arranged that he shall be so, and has provided the original sentiments as well as their translated form. As the pages of Gaffur's poems fold over the reminiscences of Hari Kumar, and they in turn are entwined in Guy Perron's thoughts of Sarah Layton, the *Quartet* comes to rest with a characteristic super-imposition of details. The centres of at least three circles have, relatively speaking, coincided. And coincidence, of this kind, is what Paul Scott's fiction is all about.

5 *Staying On* (1977)

> You have written me a love letter and I kept it under my pillow
> all night long.
>
> *Staying On*, ch. 15

At a later date, Sarah Layton marries Guy Perron and goes back
to England as his wife. Susan marries for a third time, a Scottish
doctor with whom she appears to be happy and contented. Susan
and Teddie Bingham's son has also become a doctor. These and
other snippets of information do not appear, as they would in a
Victorian or Edwardian novel, in a brief concluding chapter,
tying up all the loose ends of the story. In fact they do not appear
anywhere in the *Quartet*. Scott has circumvented the problem of
letting his readers know 'what happened' to everyone by
incorporating their later histories, briefly and tantalisingly, in the
odd corners and antechambers of another novel.

Two of the principal characters of *Staying On* are 'Tusker'
Smalley and his wife Lucy, an army couple who played very
tiny, almost walk-on parts in the *Quartet*. In the new novel we
are reminded of the parts they played. Lucy was much in
demand at the Pankot ladies' committee meetings because of her
excellent shorthand. The fact that she had had to go out to work
to acquire that proficiency, however, worked against her in the
memsahib social scene. It meant she was not quite pukka. But she
made an impression one day by remarking that Sarah Layton's
difficulties in finding a man who would 'stick' might be due to a
residual distrust of the Anglo-Indian ethos: 'She sometimes gave
this odd impression of not taking things seriously, I mean India,
us in India, and I think that's what put the young men off.' One
of the signs that Susan Layton is mentally disturbed after the
birth of her first baby is the way she is rude to the Smalleys in

church. And we remember (as Lucy does on the last page of *Staying On*) Tusker's habit of paying off the tonga wallah whenever they arrived at a party, in the hope that they would get a lift home in somebody's staff car. One night this failed to materialise and they were stranded, 'peering out into the dark waiting for transport that never turned up'. These are the incidents that light up the Smalleys as figures in the background, their characters revealed in brief anecdotes and muted parentheses.

Their association with the Laytons is commemorated in *Staying On* by a photograph of the family's farewell party in the garden of Commandant House in 1947. As well as the then Colonel Smalley and his wife, it is possible to pick out Sarah, and Guy, who had returned from Delhi before flying home to his Aunt Charlotte in England. The Smalleys, however, did not go home. They 'stayed on' in India and retired to Pankot, where they became tenants at the Lodge of Smith's Hotel. It is there that we find them, twenty-five years after Independence, at the beginning of Scott's last wonderfully comic and deeply moving novel.

It is fitting that the Laytons and the Smalleys should survive together as figures on a photograph, for the events described in the *Quartet* are here seen as in a photograph, flattened out, tidied up, and diminished. Ronald Merrick is simply the name of Susan Layton's second husband, mentioned only once in Sarah's correspondence with Lucy. Lady Manners, Daphne and Hari, have receded so far into the past as not to be noticed at all. Mirat is just the place where Susan married Teddie Bingham. And the 'awful journey to Ranpur when the train was stopped and people were killed' contains no details of Ahmed Kasim's presence there, not even his name. It is as if we were looking at the events of the *Quartet* through the wrong end of a telescope. The right end of it is trained on a future which, so far as the English in India are concerned, is bleak. Tusker and Lucy are the only permanent English residents in Pankot now. Their story is about what 'staying on' means to two people when the place in which they have stayed has declined to stay with them. Pankot has undergone traumatic changes during a quarter-century without the raj. In a way the Smalleys have altered too, in keeping with their changed fortunes and diminished expectations. But the way they have altered is not such as is best calculated to equip them for life in an ex-British hill station in Mrs Gandhi's India.

The change in Pankot is visibly demonstrated by the brand-new Shiraz hotel, dwarfing the old-fashioned comforts of Smith's with its five-storey elevation and its vistas of glass and concrete. The Smalleys' lodge, or bungalow, is in its turn dwarfed by Smith's, which is now owned by a Mrs Bhoolaboy and managed by her husband. They share the centre of the stage with the Smalleys and the Smalleys' Muslim servant, Ibrahim. Mrs Bhoolaboy's sacrifice of Smith's to buy her way into the consortium that owns the Shiraz (and other hotels in Ranpur, Mayapore and Mirat) is the trigger that sets off a chain reaction stopping only at Tusker's death and Lucy's accommodation to the facts of widowhood in what is now more than ever a strange land and a strange people.

Scott ensures that any of the cheaper kinds of narrative tension and suspense are removed from his novel by beginning it with the sentence: 'When Tusker Smalley died of a massive coronary at approximately 9.30 am on the last Monday in April 1972, his wife Lucy was out . . .'. In case we failed to register the fact, and the precision of the date, place and cause of death, the second chapter opens: 'Tusker Smalley's death can be fixed at having occurred at approximately 9.30 am rather than say twenty minutes later when the dog stopped whining and began to howl, causing Mrs Bhoolaboy to shriek, . . .'. We are informed later in this second chapter that Tusker had sustained a heart attack three months before the fatal one with which the novel opens. As a result of the importance attached to these events so early on in the story, it becomes clear that the main subject of the novel is to be the lives of Tusker and Lucy during the uneasy interval between his two heart attacks. The way the narrative works back from the second attack to the framing of Mrs Bhoolaboy's letter of eviction which caused it – and thence to other events which, whilst connected with the passing of those three vital months, spill over into the recent and then the distant past – alerts us to the manner in which the present activity of the novel subsists precariously on the shifting detritus of the past. To understand what is happening during the last three months of Tusker's and Lucy's life together we have to know not merely about their past, but about how their past informs their present, how it reinforces whatever bitterness and heartbreak attend the apparently trivial inconveniences which are the commonplaces of their lives now.

Tusker and Lucy are old people in a foreign country. (When the novel opens he is seventy, she is sixty-six.) They cannot avoid leading lives which are trivial at best and irritable most of the time. Their lives revolve around arguments as to who should exercise the dog Bloxsaw; how to deal with the weeds that are taking over the compound and choking the canna lilies; whom Lucy should invite to Tusker's birthday celebrations; and whether they can afford chicken pulao to be brought over from Smith's or should make do with a poached egg, cooked by themselves, for dinner. Events like these are punctuated by arguments with Ibrahim, arguments with the mali, arguments with Mr and Mrs Bhoolaboy, and, most often, arguments with each other. These last arguments are among the glories of the novel. Nowhere else in modern fiction – one thinks of Angus Wilson's *No Laughing Matter*, William Trevor's *The Old Boys*, Muriel Spark's *Memento Mori*, and Kingsley Amis's *Ending Up* – have I read a more compassionately accurate description of the squabbles, resentments, and mutual accusations of old people. When these squabbles are compounded of forty years living together, forty years of frustration and suspicion, the result is likely to be distressing. It can be very funny too.

Take Tusker Smalley's poached egg, for example.

The incident of the poached egg occurs in Chapter 13. Lucy has invited her Eurasian hairdresser, Susy Williams, to come to dinner with the new vicar, Father Sebastian, whom Tusker had invited the previous Sunday. In the meantime Tusker has had one of his frequent differences of opinion with Mrs Bhoolaboy, and has decided not to invest any longer in the trays of food the Smalleys have arranged to be sent over to the bungalow from Smith's. This is unfortunate today because Lucy is feeling hungry when she returns from the hairdresser and because, as she reminds him, they can hardly cater for Father Sebastian and Susy by themselves. (Their electric stove is hopelessly antiquated and inefficient.) There is a real problem lying at the back of Tusker's pig-headed decision about the dinner, but his determination to ignore the consequential difficulties – which it will be Lucy's business to circumvent – places him in a weak position when Lucy refuses to go along with his new arrangements. The tension between the Smalleys, her barely concealed bitterness and his all-too-well concealed feelings of guilt and inadequacy, are beautifully refracted through the dialogue. The beginning of the 'scene' sets the tone of all that follows:

> It was a quarter to one. At Smith's hotel, Sunday was usually chicken pulao day, and she was very hungry. She hoped Ibrahim had not been sent over for trays, because then it was difficult to get second helpings and the tray-helpings were already small enough. She poured herself a very small gin and tonic and tiptoed out to sit near Tusker and wait for him to wake up.
>
> But sitting, she saw he was awake already. His head was still lowered but his eyes were open, gazing at her.
>
> 'Hello, Tusker, dear. Have you had a nice little nap?'
>
> He did not reply. She sipped her drink. 'Would you like a little drink? A very very small gin, because it's Sunday?'
>
> 'Why because it's Sunday?'
>
> 'Sunday is chicken pulao day. Pulao goes down nicely after a spot of gin. And you have been such a good boy.'
>
> 'I'm not having chicken pulao. I'm having poached egg on toast.'
>
> 'Oh, dear. How dull. I'm not sure about egg for breakfast and egg for lunch. It's very binding. Aren't you feeling well, Tusker?'
>
> 'What I feel's neither here nor there. I'm having poached egg on toast. In fact we're both having poached egg on toast. And we're cooking them here.'
>
> She saw now that he was wearing his malevolent expression. She would have to tread carefully. 'I see,' she said. 'Are there enough eggs? . . .'

With great skill Scott has laid the fuse to his powder keg and applied his light to the end of it. The 'nice little nap', the 'the little drink', and 'A very very small gin' are verbal mannerisms (Lucy was known as 'Little Me' back in the old Pankot days) which grate on Tusker's ear. He is irritated by their tacit professions of personal unimportance and willingness to minister to grown-ups who are really no better than spoilt children. On the other hand Tusker's taciturnity, his unwillingness to explain what appears to

be a random and (in the circumstances, since Lucy is so hungry)
cruel decision, are calculated to bring out the worst in his wife.
She reveals this in a level, patient exposition of the logic of the
situation which invites replies (to blustering remarks from Tusker
that he is still master of this bloody house: 'Well? Am I or aren't
I?') like the following:

> I can't deny that. No. Indeed, I can't. You are the master of
> the house. On the other hand I am the mistress. And it is usual
> for the mistress to decide what shall be eaten and by whom and
> when, and if the master does not like it there's mostly nothing
> he can do about it unless he happens to have a talent for
> shopping and cooking which I'm afraid you haven't. I have
> seen you attempt to make a curry. In the bazaar I've known
> you squander half the week's housekeeping in half-an-hour. I
> have watched you poach an egg. If you insist on having
> poached egg for lunch I am prepared to poach it for you myself
> in order not to see several eggs wasted, and because as mistress
> of the house it's my duty to see the master fed. But after that,
> Tusker, I shall go across and have my chicken pulao. I shall
> expect to sleep between three o'clock and five o'clock and
> provided Ibrahim brings back enough eggs I may even poach
> you another one for your evening meal. Then I'll have to
> decide whether to have one too, or dine at Smith's or at the
> Club or at the Shiraz.

The careful exposition of one important and relevant aspect of
the true state of affairs is splendidly and, under the surface,
viciously, insulting. The way 'the master' is shown, in Tusker's
case, to mean little more than an incompetent layabout (in
respect of whom words like 'squander' are entirely appropriate)
is gallingly deflating. So is the flat finality of 'I have watched you
poach an egg'. And so is the conversion of 'the master' into a
parasitic and useless dog like Bloxsaw, with the admission that
'it's my duty to see the master fed'. Tusker's morose insistence
that what will be will be because he says so, and Lucy's return of
perfectly reasonable insults, can have only one conclusion:

> 'And if you say Ha! or start obfuscating and mention poached
> eggs again I shall throw this dirty pan straight at you.'

'Throw it then.'
'I shall if you say Ha!'
'Ha! Ha!'
She threw it.

The childish behaviour of both of them is expressed in a single, sudden act of frustration. Then, with the pan bouncing off Tusker 'as if he were made of something other than flesh and bone', Scott avoids that sense of self-congratulation which often attends the successful 'pulling off' of a comic effect, by gently nudging his narrative back into the past. It is the past as seen by Lucy, calling to mind the only other occasion on which she had hit her husband. This turns out to be not entirely to Tusker's discredit, when she compares him, as he was then, with the new cosmopolitan executives who were also involved. And so we are returned to a new phase of the scene in the kitchen of the bungalow, and a new argument conducted on a slightly different basis. At the end of it (though there never is an end of it, really – and that is one of the facts of life this novel so sensitively reproduces) the argument of the poached eggs is closed, in an appropriately surly, but for the time being final way:

She drank what was left of her gin and got up.
'Where are you going?'
'I am going to scramble your egg.'
'I don't want an egg now. I'm past eating.'

Elsewhere the comedy is often of a broader kind, though invariably it takes notice of the serious ambitions and anxieties of those who create it. A good example is Scott's handling of Tusker's first heart attack, which happens while he is on the lavatory in the bathroom/w.c. The details of his position, slumped half-on half-off one of the two 'viceregal thrones' the Smalleys have installed in the bungalow, calls for an explanation of the bizarre sleeping and toilet arrangements which a combination of Mrs Bhoolaboy's miserliness and their own sense of decorum has forced on the Smalleys. This comic surround to a desperately serious situation is compounded by Ibrahim's circumstances when called upon to render assistance. He is

approaching the climactic moment of his sexual congress with
Minnie, one of the maids at Smith's (and incidentally, in the past,
Sarah and Susan Layton's little ayah): ' "Coming, Memsahib!"
he cried when he realised who it was. The overstatement of the
week.' And so Ibrahim carries Tusker back to his bed, amid silent
speculations about lavatories and English bathing habits. It is the
sort of situation that would appeal to Anthony Powell's feeling for
the petty incongruities of life, and which he would have refined at
least half-way out of existence. But Scott manages to avoid both
understatement and vulgarity in his handling of the scene. It is
rounded off with one of those poetic-prosaic touches he applies so
well:

> Ibrahim murmured, 'Ibrahim dossing down in living-room
> rest of night, keeping watch. Memsahib sleeping.'
>   Curled up in a blanket in front of the fireplace which was
> still warm with the embers of the pine-log fire lit that evening
> he kept nodding off. Whenever he woke he crept into the
> bedroom. She had kept her bedside light on, but covered the
> shade with a cloth. There was just sufficient light to see that all
> was well, that both slept: Memsahib upright against her piled-
> up pillow, under that cascade of cobwebbed net playing in her
> dreams, perhaps, Miss Havisham in Great Expectations, still
> waiting for her groom.
>   At 5.00 am he kicked out the last spark of the wood fire in
> case at dawn there was a mysterious association of ideas and
> The Lodge burnt down because she had dreamed it. (ch. 3)

Poetic, because of the image of Lucy as Miss Havisham under the
cascade of the cobwebbed net – a Miss Havisham, though, who
has secured, not lost, the husband who, now, she is near the point
of losing for ever. Prosaic, because Ibrahim has no knowledge of
Dickens's novel outside the film of it he must have seen at the
Electric Cinema in Pankot or the Odeon at Finsbury Park. And if
Lucy was dreaming of Miss Havisham, she too would be
dreaming of the film, the cosmetic version. Like Ibrahim, she is
an inveterate cinema-goer. Even here, though, there is poetry of
a kind. The insistence on 'playing' the part of Dickens's heroine
reminds us that Lucy had always wanted to play a part on the
stage, but was always prevented from doing so by nervousness

and the gift she has always possessed of never being in the right place at the right time.

The least complex type of comedy, the type that suggests least about the sadness and unsatisfactoriness of life, is exemplified in a scene in which Lucy tries to tell Ibrahim that she needs a boy to attend to the garden whilst Tusker is recovering from his heart attack. Lucy's choice of words does not help to clarify her intention. She speaks of 'procuring' the boy, 'confessing everything when the Sahib is well again', and, best of all, proposes that the boy should be 'not mine alone, Ibrahim. Ours. Yours and mine. Couldn't we between us find and use such a boy? . . . I mean he could be of service to you too, in odd ways.' Coming immediately after Ibrahim's interrupted performance with Minnie on the charpoy, Lucy's ambiguous suggestions about the boy (and she is a vicar's daughter) are comically inappropriate to both mistress and servant. This broad verbal comedy is provided with a descriptive counterpoint in the scene where Mr Bhoolaboy (who is a very thin, insignificant-looking man) wakes up one morning to find the mountainous folds of Mrs Bhoolaboy's flesh pinning him to the bed in an unaccustomed, and by now quite unconscious, amorous embrace. Scott's painstaking and detailed description of Mr Bhoolaboy's escape from imminent suffocation, without waking his wife in the process, is one of the high points of vulgar comedy in this novel.

Whilst *Staying On* is in much of its detail a very funny novel, its overall effect is one of profound sadness. With all its comic strengths, and its sophisticated documentation of the new Indian class structure (much more convincing, because less preoccupied with a relatively small stratum of the new society, than the novels of Ruth Prawer Jhabvala), this novel's principal claim on our attention arises from the extent to which it makes us care about the fortunes of the people in it. These are Tusker and Lucy especially, but also a large cast of secondary (and tertiary) characters who include not merely Ibrahim and Mr Bhoolaboy, but Susy, Minnie, Joseph (the new mali) – even Mr Pandey, Mrs Bhoolaboy's accountant, and Coocoo Menektara, the senior regimental officer's wife. In so far as our attention is absorbed by the Smalleys, the effect produced by Tusker's death at the end of the book has something in common with what we feel when Judy collapses into chronic alcoholism in Brian Moore's *Judith Hearne*,

or when Mohun Biswas dies in his house in Sikkim Street in V. S.
Naipaul's *A House for Mr Biswas*. All three of them are deeply
moving incidents that emphasise the seriousness of the efforts a
human being might make to stand for something, to *be* something, and to be worth something in his own right. In *Staying On*
the cause of our sadness is closely related to a view of life that
Scott has entertained over the whole course of his writing career.
The Smalleys illustrate it in their own very distinctive way. But at
different times in their careers Johnnie Brown, Dorothy Gower,
William Conway and Edward Thornhill experienced a desolation which had something in common with the desolation that
exists at the centre of Tusker's and Lucy's lives and that, in their
case, no change in their circumstances can drive away.

'I have had rather a sad life . . . Yes, from the beginning I had
a sad life,' Lucy says to herself as she seals her letter to Sarah
Layton. 'A life like a flower that has never bloomed, but how
many do?' Certainly her own life cannot be said to have bloomed.
It had been given no romantic nourishment from Tusker after his
pre-marital visits to the solicitors' office where she used to work in
London. At that time he offered her the dreams a young
inexperienced rector's daughter might long for in the person of a
young officer, a stranger from the mysterious East. But her
dreams withered with the clumsiness and infrequency of his
sexual possession of her. Her dreamless days were stultified by the
routine and hierarchy of Anglo-Indian military life, the weakness
of her husband's ambition and, finally, the uselessness of any
ambition he might still have nurtured after 1947 and
Independence. Having stayed on into the sixties and early
seventies, she has had to make the sharp adjustment from being a
colonel's wife in the British army to being a person whose role is
negligible or simply non-existent.

The Anglo-Indian community which has deserted Pankot and
Ranpur has been replaced by 'a new race of sahibs and
memsahibs of international status and connexion . . . and Lucy
and Tusker had become for them almost as far down the social
scale as the Eurasians were in the days of the raj.' The new race is
represented by Tusker's employers in the pharmaceutical company he joined after his retirement from the army – people like
Sigrid Poppadoum, a tall Swedish beauty married to a 'prickly
little Indian husband . . . who could steer government contracts

the way of Feibergerstein and Smith, Brown and Mackintosh'. Now, in 1972, they are represented in the Smalleys' personal lives by members of the new Indian entrepreneurial class like Mrs Bhoolaboy and Mr and Mrs Desai, 'the emerging Indian middle class of wheelers and dealers who with their chicanery, their corrupt practices, their black money, their use of political power for personal gain were ruining the country or if not ruining it making it safe chiefly for themselves'. Their symbol is the Shiraz hotel, and their stranglehold over the old India is demonstrated in their conspiracy with Mrs Bhoolaboy, to take over Smith's in order to raze it to the ground and extend their own monstrous building. The Smalleys, Mr Bhoolaboy, Ibrahim and Joseph are simply nuisances who will have to be got out of the way.

The same thing is happening in the Church where Mr Bhoolaboy, who has been a churchwarden at Saint John's for more years than he can remember, is being pushed to one side by a new dispensation. This is headed by Father Sebastian, a very dark-skinned Southern Indian, whose attitude to the Church is demonstrated by his facility in channelling funds from Ranpur to Pankot. By doing this the new rector performs miracles of technological wizardry that eventually get the old organ (the one Mr Maybrick used to play in the days of the raj) back into full working order. Lucy Smalley is unwittingly involved in what Father Sebastian obviously thinks of as a charming anachronism, when she has her photograph taken with Mr Bhoolaboy and Joseph at the grave of Mabel Layton – a photograph which is to illustrate 'an article I am doing for a magazine in Madras which finds its way all over the world'.

Lucy is not the only person in the novel to feel that whatever was desirable in the past (which is mainly, as she knows, a romantic vision of what the past might have been) is being destroyed by forces in the present which she is incapable of understanding, let alone coming to terms with. Mr Bhoolaboy feels the same about his hotel, which has never been a mere business proposition to him, but a place which has to keep its goodwill through skilful management and diplomatic human relations. Too late he discovers 'I have only been caretaker of a development site.' Ibrahim regrets the passing of the raj because, under Colonel and Mrs Moxon-Greife, 'the servants were treated as members of the family, entitled to their good humours and bad humours, their sulks, their outbursts of temper, their right to show who is really boss, their right to their discreetly appropriated perks, the feathers they had to provide for the nest when the nest they presently inhabited was abandoned by homeward bound employers.'

But the full impact of the change is felt by no one more than by the Smalleys. They have made different investments in India, or so they feel, but in each case the new India has let them down. In Lucy's case, though, the heights from which she has descended are largely fictional. It is true that, at the very end, later than she had ever hoped, she became a colonel's wife. But the years before that were filled with disappointment and chagrin. Tusker's lack of ambition had ensured that even when he was promoted, to major, and then to lieutenant-colonel, the wives of other majors and lieutenant-colonels would leave her in no doubt that she and her husband were the junior, because most recent, members of that particular 'club'. The pain this constant assumption of inferiority has caused her, and the bitterness towards Tusker it has left her with, are harshly illuminated by her behaviour after his recovery from his first heart attack. She is terrified about what her financial position will be if he dies first. In a desperate attempt to get him to explain what provision, if any, he has made against such an eventuality, she lets fly at him all the resentment she feels about the past. Her frenzied diatribe is not brought to any speedier conclusion by a jibe Tusker is stupid enough to make about her shorthand. She reminds him that she was proud to have acquired that skill, even though in India it marked her out as a girl who had once had to work for a living:

And it came in handy enough, didn't it? Without it, the cost of discovering one had married a man without manly ambition might have proved insupportable. Every hour you spent hiding yourself behind a desk, Tusker, was paid for by me in little humiliations, dogsbodying for the wives of the men who profited from the work that flowed from your desk, your desks, your hundreds of desks, none of which any man who thought as much of his wife as he thought of his own peace of mind and comfort of body would have sat at for a moment once he realised that other men were enjoying the fruits of his work and their wives with them and his own wife suffering. It was you,

Tusker, who made me a dogsbody because a role of dogsbody
for yourself was the one you had chosen to play.   (ch. 7)

Then Tusker made things worse by 'freaking out' as soon as he
left the army, behaving like a man who held the army and all it
stood for in contempt. So Lucy was let down by Tusker in his
behaviour both in the army and out of it. This is the past of which
she regrets the passing, just as at an earlier time it was to be the
future into which she was proud and excited to enter, after her
vicarage wedding and her humdrum life at the office. She
imagined fellow-officers 'standing to make a little roof of crossed
swords over our heads', and a Maharajah as a guest, 'with pearls
looped round his neck and the Star of India on his turban'. None
of these things materialised. In fact life in India was every bit as
depressing and diminishing as life in England had been. The
trouble was, 'I've always had this tendency to imagine, to
fantasise, to *project*'. But there was nothing substantial to project
her imagination on to, or, now, to reflect it back against – except
a picture of army life in Pankot and elsewhere from which the
petty humiliations and embarrassments had been removed, and
the life of a typical pukka memsahib substituted for them. In her
less self-deceiving moments she knows that the life she and Tusker
led before 1947 was much too like the life they are having to live
after it. The deterioration in their finances makes a difference,
though, and so does the fact that the people who now look down
on her and Tusker now are not white, but brown.

None of these things would have been significant if Lucy could
have depended on Tusker. But the novel shows how during the
period between his first and his fatal heart attack Tusker
persistently lets her down; and then behaves badly as a response
to her behaving badly over being let down. Her efforts to provide
a mali who will appear to be paid by Mrs Bhoolaboy instead of by
herself, so that in his own eyes Tusker will not have lost face, are
greeted with a complete lack of response, an unwillingness even
to notice that the mali is there. Having invited the new rector to
dinner at the bungalow, he makes no attempt to help Lucy
arrange for the visit. Instead he throws up difficulty after
difficulty, as if he had no responsibility in the matter. His
treatment of Ibrahim nearly loses them their only servant at a
time when to possess at least one servant is crucial. But

underneath his apparent boorishness and insensitivity to his wife
there festers a deep sense of guilt at the way she has been treated
which he has never been able to confess to her, and which has
exacerbated rather than softened his emotional brutality.

It is therefore of great importance to Lucy that her anxieties
about her financial position at Tusker's death do at least elicit a
letter from him which contains a statement of the appropriate
details. What is important is not the information about the
money (which does not give many grounds for optimism) but the
fact that Tusker did write to her, and, from her point of view, in
astonishing terms. His explanation of what has happened to the
money brings with it a much wider explanation of his failure to
provide Lucy with what he knew she wanted, but which he knew
it was not in him to achieve:

> I still think we were right to stay on, though I don't think of it
> any longer as staying on, but just as hanging on, which people
> of our age and upbringing and limited talents, people who
> have never been really poor but never had any real money,
> never inherited real money, never made real money, have to
> do, wherever they happen to be, when they can't work any
> more. I'm happier hanging on in India, not for India as India
> but because I can't just merely think of it as a place where I
> drew my pay for the first 25 years of my working life, which is a
> hell of a long time anyway, though by rights it should have
> been longer. But there you are. Suddenly the powers that be
> say, Right, Smalley, we're not wanted here any more, we've all
> got to bugger off, too bad you're not ten years younger or ten
> years older. I thought about this a lot at the time and it seemed
> to me I'd invested in India, not money which I've never had,
> not talent (Ha!) which I've only had a limited amount of,
> nothing India needed or needs or has been one jot the better
> for, but was all I had to invest in anything. Me. Where I went
> wrong was in thinking of it that way and expecting a return on
> the investment in the end, and anticipating the profits . . .
>   (ch. 14)

His situation has something in common with George Spruce's in
The Bender: limited talent and meagre finances discourage
ambition and produce a willingness to settle for mere security.

But apart from the difference in age and geography, there is also the difference that George's wife divorced him whereas Lucy and Tusker stayed married. There is also the difference that through all the humiliations and vexations Lucy and Tusker have grown together, as well as apart. The letter Tusker has written, blessedly, at the eleventh hour, makes it clear to Lucy that this is how he sees it: 'You've been a good woman to me, Luce. Sorry I've not made it clear I think so.' They are sentences that give Lucy something to hold on to, that show her that her life with Tusker has not been totally useless and empty. When she goes to sleep on the night before his death, 'Peace enveloped her. She turned on her side away from the light from the living-room and let her sleepy fingers find their way to the envelope that contained the only love letter she had had in all the years she had lived.'

The light from the living-room shows that Tusker has returned from the Club with Dr and Mrs Mitra. The next time we see it is after Tusker's death, when Lucy needs Ibrahim and Minnie to sleep in the living-room next door. Now the only light comes from the empty bedroom, at 3.30 in the morning. Lucy has awakened and needs to go into the kitchen. In the living-room she is able to make out three figures:

> Curled up near the almost dead fire were two shapes in blankets. Minnie and Ibrahim, one on each side of the fireplace. Going gently past them she caught her breath because there was a third shape, huddled with its back to the wall.
> Joseph.
> The three of them.   (ch. 16)

A flicker of amusement at the chastely decorous sleeping arrangements of Minnie and Ibrahim soon gives way to an oppressive sadness. Three dispossessed Indians at the feet of their near-destitute mistress; and her only comfort a letter and a succession of severely edited memories. Of all Paul Scott's many images of spiritual desolation this one is among the bleakest. For Lucy, 'staying on' has become an even more permanent and hopeless condition than it had seemed to be during those twenty-five years with Tusker. The comic mood has entirely evaporated,

Index

Fictional characters and places are indicated by single quotation marks. Abbreviated titles of the novel(s) in which they appear are placed in square brackets. Most of these abbreviations are unambiguous: D.Sc = *The Day of the Scorpion*; D.Sp = *A Division of the Spoils*.

'Coomer, Harry', see Kumar, Hari
Corrida at San Feliu, The, 3; 6, 22, 29, 39–40, 41, 57–64, 86, 112
'Craddock, Bruce and Thelma' [*CSF*], 57–60, 62–3
'Craig, Esther' [*MW*], 32
'Craig, Major' [*MW*], 7, 31–9 *passim*
'Crane, Edwina' [*RQ*], 8, 9, 17, 66–7, 69–70, 81–2, 85, 93, 98
'Cranston, Jim' [*BP*], 48, 54, 56
Cripps, Sir Stafford (Cripps Offer), 19, 73

'Daintree, Dr' [*BP*], 48, 54, 56
'Darshansingh' [*CSF*], 3
'Dass, Havildar' [*JC*], 14
Day of the Scorpion, The, iii, 4–5, 31, 65, 67–9, 74, 84–5, 87–90, 92, 93
Delhi, 104
'Desai, Mr and Mrs' [*SO*], 113
'Dibrapur', 66, 82
Dickens, Charles, *Great Expectations*, 110
Don Quixote, 41
Durrell, Lawrence, *The Alexandria Quartet*, 95
Dyer, General R.E.H., 75

'Elephant Hill' [*MW*], 32–3, 35
Encounter, see Beloff, Max
Eurasian themes in P. Scott's novels, *see* Scott, Paul

Faena, 61
'Feibergerstein and Smith, Brown and Mackintosh' [*SO*], 113
Forster, E. M., *A Passage to India*, 16–17, 65, 82, 94

'Gaffur' [*RQ*], 99, 100–2
Gandhi, Mrs Indira, 105
'Gopalakand, Nawab of' [*BP*, *D.Sp*], 25
'Gower, Dorothy' [*AS*], 20–5 *passim*, 112
'Gower, Tom' [*AS*], 20–5 *passim*
'Graystone's Valley' [*CLP*], 45

'Hakinawa, Lieutenant' [*CLP*], 43, 45–6
'Heaslop, Ronnie' (in E. M. Forster's *A Passage to India*), 16
Hemingway, Ernest, 58
'Hurst, Alan' [*MC*], 26–9 *passim*
'Hurst, Edward' [*MC*], 26–9 *passim*
'Hurst, Mrs' [*MC*], 26–9 *passim*
'Hurst, Stella' [*MC*], 27, 29

'Ibrahim' [*SO*], 105–6, 109, 111, 113, 115, 117
Imphal, 31
India, Independence of, 5, 19–20, 52–3, 66, 72–3, 84, 104–5, 112–16
Indian Mutiny, 79
Indian National Army, 70

Jewel in the Crown, The, ix, 42, 66–7, 77, 79–83, 84, 85–6, 94, 97–8, 99
Jhabvala, Ruth Prawer, 111
Johnnie Sahib, x, 3, 11–19, 21, 39, 112
'Johns, Lieutenant' [*JS*], 19
'Joseph' [*SO*], 111, 113
'Jundapur' [*BP*], 49, 51, 54–6, 77, 100

'Kalipur' [*AS*], 25
'Kandipat' [*D.Sc*], 67
Kashmir, 68
'Kasim, Ahmed' [*RQ*], 69, 71, 75, 93, 101, 104
'Kasim, Muhammed' [*RQ*], 70, 73
'Kasim, Sayed' [*D.Sp*], 70
'Khan, Muzzafir' [*RQ*], 70, 87
Khudabad, 38
'Kinwar' [*BP*], 49–50, 67–8
Kipling, Rudyard, xi, 6
'Krishanramarao' [*BP*], 42, 49–51
'Kumar, Hari' [*RQ*], 22, 67–9, 75–91 *passim*, 93–8 *passim*, 101–2, 104

Larkin, Philip, ix
'Layton, Colonel John' [*RQ*], 70–1, 87